DEDI

I dedicate this book to the many past academic authors who have edited, coached, tutored, mentored, and encouraged through the process of editing and revising their masters and doctoral publications. I am grateful for your trust in me, and the many wonderful referrals to me to assist other university students with their academic journeys. May each of you continued to be blessed

My hope is that the information in this book can help guide the future scholars, for whom I wrote this book. Please feel free to reach out to me for assistance—my job is to be here for you and to help you succeed—and **Keep it Simple, Scholars!**

MW00958909

PREFACE

In all the years of editing for peers and as part of my normal job duties it never occurred to me to edit professionally until the last year of my doctoral program at University of Phoenix. I gladly assisted my cohorts, since their success was my success. That is how I look at what I do as a certified copyeditor: A thesis or dissertation is the epitome of one's livelihood; there are promotions and raises to be earned with the attainment of a post-graduate degree. Yet, my perception of a student's paper is not a boon of getting rich or providing sub-standard services:

My goal is to have students submit a paper that I would be proud of submitting for a degree if the paper were mine! No longer are scholars bound by brick-and-mortar campuses or in-person lectures and meeting with mentors and committee members. However, the journey is still a singular accomplishment from the student perspective. Sitting in a room, staring at a computer, reading numerous articles, taking notes, getting frustrated, forgetting to eat, sleep, exercise, or socialize—yes, I have been down your path.

Some final advice for all students is to realize that the thesis and dissertation journey has changed over the years. Be your own advocate! At residencies, download every file, every document, every presentation. They may only be available during residency but could be valuable later on in your journey! For encouragement and support from others on the same journey as you, join scholarly social media groups for support and networking, and exchange information with your cohorts and keep in touch with each other—perhaps even graduate together!

<u>Keep it Simple, Scholars!</u>

CONTENTS

Acknowledgments .... Pg i

Foreword .... Pg ii

1   Expectations for Using this Resource .... Pg 1

2   Overview: Proposal, Dissertation, Thesis .... Pg 4

3   Mentor-Mentee and Committee Relationship ... Pg 7

4   Getting Started: Choosing Your Topic .... Pg 11

5   Chapter 2: Why Write the Literature Review First ... Pg 14

6   Basic Elements of Chapter 1: The Introduction to the Study ... Pg 17

7   The "Recipe" Chapter 3: Method .... Pg 23

8   The Finishing Touch: Chapter 4: Findings & Chapter 5: Conclusions, Implications, & Recommendations For Further Research ... Pg 36

9   Write Like a Scholar: Basic Editing Issues .... Pg 40

10 Plagiarism, Citations, & References .... Pg 60

11 Ethics of Using Outside Assistance .... Pg 64

12 What's Next For You? .... Pg 71

References .... Pg 75

Appendixes .... Pg 79

Appendix A: Resource Examples .... Pg 80

Appendix B: Committee Member Request Example ... Pg 81

Appendix C: Prospectus Outline Example .... Pg 83

Appendix D: Research Plan Example   Pg 91

Appendix E: Dissertation Format Example   Pg 112

Appendix F: List of Possible Required Documents   Pg 144

Appendix G: Participant Withdrawal Example   Pg 145

Appendix H: Field Test Feedback Example   Pg 146

Appendix I: Letter of Recruitment Example   Pg 148

About the Author   Pg 150

Index   Pg 151

ACKNOWLEDGMENTS

I would like to recognize the champion of every decision I have made over the past several years, my husband, Eric Conzelmann, whose love, encouragement, and support have been offered so thoughtfully and generously in my every endeavor.

There are two people whom I want to thank for their friendship and believing in my editorial skills, so much so, that these two individuals were the guiding force in my starting to edit professionally: Dr. Laurie Brunson, and Dr. Maria Schellhase. Dr. Laurie, your struggle to become a doctor of management was frustrating and encouraging; you never let the hurdles stop you! You were my first official doctoral client, and I was proud to assist you right through to the formatting of your dissertation for publication! Dr. Maria, your many invitations to visit "Hoover Dam" was well placed, and several times, I was ready to take you up on that offer! Now that we know we did not need to "take the plunge," we are both here to help and inspire up-and-coming academics on their journeys—so they may not need to take that plunge either!

Additional thanks to Dr. Laurie Brunson and Dr. Von Perot for generously sharing some of the editorial issues in their draft dissertations as examples for up-and-coming scholars. Thank you to Julie Clockston for offering feedback on this book and Stephanie Cope, who read and used the book, and provided additional feedback on the ease of read, understanding, and use prior to publication.

Thank you, scholars, all for your generous support and kindness!

FOREWORD

Spring is in bloom and I cannot help to think about the trees that are struggling to flourish throughout the ongoing drought in northern California. In my community of Amador County, many scrub oak trees survive through four seasons of little or no rain. Below these majestic trees lives an intricate root system. Developing from a small acorn the initial taproot seeks a dependable source of moisture, minerals, and nutrients that follow the deeply rooted paths of previous or adjoining trees. This lateral root growth will continue through the lifetime of the tree, weaving and grafting with other roots to provide an anchor of health and strength for the trees. Just as the root of the oak tree relies on the previous pathways of other oaks to survive, my path to a completed dissertation took me on a personal and profession journey that included an intertwining anchor of strength from my editor, Dr. Julie Conzelmann.

Just like the mighty oak, the 15 peers in our 3rd year University of Phoenix residency class looked to each other and our instructor for an opportunity to understand the journey we were about to take, writing our proposal. Although many of my peers seemed to understand the path forward only one stood out as fully understanding what was needed and willing to share what she had learned, Julie Conzelmann. During residency, Julie was quick to understand both the necessary concepts and structures for the initial proposal and the beginnings of Chapters 1 through 3. During the last day of residency, our group decided to create a doctoral Facebook page, which Dr. Conzelmann moderates!

All seemed to be going well but as a doctoral candidate do not fool yourself, it is a journey both personally and professionally. Over the course of the next year, I stumbled in my dissertation process with many personal issues such as my father, his brother, and father-in-law's passing, recessional business bankruptcy, a three-year Internal Revenue Service (IRS) audit, my health issues and my husband's alcoholism, drug dependency, and recovery. By my third year residency, I was exhausted and barely able to sit through class or interact with my peers. Julie consoled me during third year, even bringing me a hand crocheted blanket to wrap around me during class to stay warm. She truly was my tentacle for health and survival.

Although there was not a race to graduate, Dr. Conzelmann, even through her own personal journey, finished well ahead of many of our peers with humility, warmth, and a willingness to help others. An already excellent writer, Dr. Conzelmann explored the notion of becoming an editor. Since I was on the tortoise track for completion, Dr. Conzelmann asked if I would be her first client. Through the doctoral Facebook page, she assisted by providing files for the most recent university instructions, documents, and the personal support needed to complete my journey. As time went on, Dr. Conzelmann opened her editing business to assist other master's and doctoral students; she quickly gained a significant number of students in different stages of their studies. I finally graduated in 2015. I can attest that I would not have finished without Dr. Conzelmann as my editor and colleague!

I applaud Dr. Conzelmann for compiling the information contained in her book ***Keep it Simple, Scholars!*** Dr. Conzelmann has the lived personal experience of writing dissertations, theses, and books; and through this book, provides answers to many of the questions that a student will have in their writing experience. Additionally, Dr. Conzelmann is a certified copyeditor, editing children's books, journal articles, novels, and hundreds of quantitative, qualitative, and mixed method dissertations and theses, making her well qualified to provide the most updated academic writing and editing assistance.

Keep it Simple, Scholars! provides a gold mine of dissertation and thesis assistance to students struggling with their writing, editing, or formatting. The 12 chapters in this book are replete with both effective information for the reader and strategies to assist the student with completing their dissertation or thesis. Dr. Conzelmann relates her vast experience editing for students attending over 20 universities worldwide in Chapter 1, outlining the expectations of the book as a resource. Chapter 2 provides the definitions and overview of the contents of a proposal, dissertation, and thesis.

Particularly useful is Chapter 3, offering a description of the mentor, committee, and mentee relationship. Dr. Conzelmann provides outstanding advice for selecting your mentor and committee members, and student's responsibilities during the dissertation and thesis writing journey. The most difficult task, where to begin, takes center stage in Chapter 4 providing assistance in narrowing the topic of study.

The literature review is the central topic in Chapter 5. Dr. Conzelmann offers information about both recommendations and content as well as the type of sources to include in a dissertation or theses. Chapter 6 contains information that is useful for writing Chapter 1 of your study. The basic framework is included along with the essential sections and basic elements included for the student.

Chapter 7 describes the "Recipe Method" for writing the method section of your paper. This chapter is especially useful as a summary of research design and appropriateness and the ingredients of what should be contained in Chapter 3 of your study. Chapter 8 contains the truly exciting part of a research study,: An explanation of what should be contained in Chapter 4, the results and findings! A brief overview of what should be contained in Chapter 4 and Chapter 5 of a dissertation or theses is included.

Chapter 9 contains one of the most important parts of writing a research study, writing like a scholar. This chapter provides tips on typical editing issues Dr. Conzelmann has experienced over the period of her editing career. Do you want to find out when to use *affect* or *effect*? Chapter 9 provides the answer!

At all universities, using someone else's work as your own is a serious offense. Chapter 10 clarifies the different types of plagiarism, and an explanation of citations and references. Sometimes a student may need assistance in the area of editing or statistical analysis. Chapter 11 provides a summary of the ethical use of help beyond your mentor and committee members. Many new businesses and individuals are more than willing to take your money to help students complete a dissertation or theses. Dr. Conzelmann shows her expertise in this area and provides excellent advice on using outside assistance. This book ends with a chapter about what to do after completing a dissertation or theses. Now that you are a scholar, many different options are available!

I am so pleased that Dr. Conzelmann put this book together; truly gifted individuals make a difference in the world. This book provides a deep-rooted layer of suggestions weaved from the experiences of others to help scholars grow during the dissertation or thesis journey.

Dr. Laurie Brunson
February 2016
Jackson, California

CHAPTER 1

EXPECTATIONS FOR USING THIS RESOURCE

Generally, your university, mentor, and committee members should provide you with specific guidelines, documents, and tools you will need to complete your thesis or dissertation. For the this book, most of the information provided in the text follows the American Psychological Association (APA) manual, Sixth Edition (2009). The same basic information is applicable to the Modern Language Association (MLA) Handbook for Writers of Research Papers, Seventh Edition (2009), and Chicago Manual of Style (CMS) (2010) formats for academic papers. While formatted examples are provided in this book, none is adopted fully in these formats by any university, but is for use by you as a guide. Be sure to obtain a physical copy of any writing style manual you need and review the rules often in accordance with the editing and formatting requirements for your particular university.

I also suggest having several other reference books on hand. First, the McGraw-Hill Handbook of English Grammar and Usage, Second Edition (2013) is a wonderful source of assistance with grammatical issues. When the reviewers come back and note you use too many pronouns, you can use the index in the back of the book to look up pronouns, and discover how you can revise your writing to meet university requirements. Second, the Merriam-Webster's Collegiate Dictionary, Eleventh Edition (2014) can be very helpful for defining words, and to research if some words are accurate for use in a statement. Third, obtaining a copy of The Oxford Essential Guide to Writing (Kane, 1988) has a variety of writing tools, from who to organize your writing, style and technique, and punctuation and grammar, all of which can help you write and refine your work. Fourth, Garner's Modern American Usage (Garner, 2009) is also a great companion book to the Oxford book listed above—but has more information about grammar and style. Finally, a great resource is Dissertations and Theses from Start to Finish: Psychology and Related Fields, Second Edition (Cone & Foster, 2006). I found this book highly helpful while writing my dissertation. Many of these Resource Examples are listed in Appendix A or in the References for this book.

Many other resources are available and you should strive to learn to write well and edit your work using the tools and guides available to you for much less than the cost of editing, tutoring, and coaching. The effort you put into writing and editing your own work will continue into your future endeavors to write books, articles, and work-related documents.

The resources, document examples, or other suggestions provided in this book are not exclusive to any specific university thesis or dissertation requirements, elements or guidelines. Again, as the academic author, it is imperative you determine what documents you need to conduct your study, and work with your chair and committee within university parameters to meet the ethical needs for your specific research.

Some final thoughts as you move forward toward earning your master's or doctoral degree: Have the necessary technology required for your degree program. Be sure to have one or two external drives available as backup for saving your extremely important documents. Save your documents daily, especially if you walk away from your computer! Some people e-mail the last draft of their document to a separate e-mail account or save their files to Dropbox or the Cloud. These are great resources!

Buy and maintain a reliable computer. Install the necessary software for your course and research needs. Create a backup plan for emergencies, system failures, viruses, and crashes. Having both a laptop and desktop computer are ideal, in the event you might travel away from home. Libraries are also a great resource if a computer is not available to you.

This book is not an all-inclusive guide for all resources, writing, tutoring, coaching, transcription, statistical, or editorial issues. The use of an experienced and certified editor may still be necessary; although, using this book as a guide, and obtaining any of the aforementioned resources, should help save students time and money and help you **Keep it Simple, Scholars!**

CHAPTER 2

OVERVIEW: PROPOSAL, DISSERTATION, THESIS

What is a Proposal?

According to Cone and Foster (2006), an academic proposal is a fully written document containing at least three chapters of well-written and organized information about a topic of research. The organization of the chapters involves listing topical information in a logical order, much like a recipe. List the chapters in numerical order, and by various overarching topics, as follows.

Chapter 1, introduces the topic, and a brief overview of the research development process including the problem, purpose, significance, theoretical or conceptual framework, research question, either sub-question or hypotheses, nature of the study, assumptions, definitions of terms, scope, limitations, delimitations, and a summary.

Chapter 2 is a fully written and organized review of the existing literature regarding the topic, with a CLEAR section describing the GAP in the literature, and the impetus for conducting the study.

Chapter 3 is a fully written, detailed, and well-organized review of the research method, design, and full process: geographical location, sample population, type of sampling, informed consent, confidentiality, instrumentation, data collection, pilot or field test, data analysis, validity or confirmability. The information about YOUR study is written in the future tense, all cited material is written in the past tense (John explained the problem.), not PASSIVE VOICE (John said the problem could be explained).

What is a Dissertation?

A dissertation encompasses all three of the chapters provided for the proposal, revised to be ALL in past tense, not passive voice, with the addition of Chapter 4 and Chapter 5 (Cone & Foster, 2006). The last two chapters conclude the dissertation, providing the findings from the research study and conclusions and implications from conducting the study.

Chapter 4 should ONLY be a full review of what occurred when you performed your study. Do not include any cited material from your literature review; only snippets of quotes from your participants to substantiate your findings is allowed and NOT the FULL VERBATIM transcripts. The transcripts should NEVER be seen by anyone other than you, as the researcher, and a transcriptionist, who also needs to provide a non-disclosure agreement (refer to your Collaborative Institutional Training Initiative (CITI) or human research ethics training).

Chapter 5 is a review of the findings of Chapter 4 wherein you may substantiate your findings with literature AND quotes from your participants, relate the conclusions one could draw from the findings, and the implications of the findings to your target audience (from Chapter 1), and recommendations for other researchers to carry your research further.

What is a Thesis?

A thesis is the same as a dissertation, encompassing at least five chapters. The writing and research should be at the same scholarly level; however, the student may only be obtaining a master's degree, rather than a dissertation.

There is a variety of resources for creating dissertations and theses, for this chapter, much of the information is from Cone and Foster (2006) and my personal experience writing my dissertation. Many of the cited the sources in this book are available through websites and bookstores. It is important to take the time to discover which books your university expects you to use as guides, and to obtain a guide specific to your university to help you **Keep it Simple, Scholars!** in all your educational endeavors!

CHAPTER 3

MENTOR-MENTEE AND COMMITTEE RELATIONSHIP

Generally, your university, mentor, and committee members should provide you with specific guidelines about the tools you will need to complete your thesis or dissertation. However, no one can provide you with everything you need to be successful; thus, I have compiled some ideas here I used for my own doctoral journey. Remember to gauge your relationships with your mentor and committee members to meet your needs and goals—that is, this is YOUR journey, not theirs.

Questions your Mentor/Committee Members Might Ask

When you reach the point in your journey where you choose your mentor (if your masters or doctoral program includes you selecting a mentor), they will want some specific information from you. You need to be prepared to provide this information. The prospective mentor may ask you for information. The 10 most prevalent questions a mentor or committee member might ask you include:

1. Why did you choose this particular topic?

2. How well do you write?

3. If you chose a research design, which one did you choose. Why did you choose the one you did and not the other?

4. Do you have a prospectus or proposal in process; if so, would you share it with me?

5. How well do you believe you can work on this project on your own?

6. How familiar are you with the method and design you chose for your research?

7. Are you familiar with the required writing and formatting style; if not, will you obtain the necessary information so you can increase your skills in this area?

8. Have you selected committee members?

9. What type of and how often do you expect feedback during this project? (Check availability in or out of class, this is important!)

10. What do you plan to do once you complete your degree?

Remember that you are looking for the best mentor and a good fit for guidance and encouragement on this journey. Be honest with your responses. Take time to review these questions and jot down your answers for interviews with prospective mentors! It will be helpful to do the research and have quick and accurate responses! If you are having difficulties in some of these areas, you could state that your hope is for the mentor to assist you with obtaining a better understanding of the concepts—letting them know you will value their advice and expertise!

Questions you should ask your Mentor and Committee Members

Although this is YOUR journey, your committee members are your guides for meeting the content requirements for a thesis or dissertation. It is only fair that each of you knows where you stand in the process. You should be prepared to ask your prospective mentor and committee members some questions, too!

1. Do you have a specialization in any of the following: my topic, research method, research design, statistical, or qualitative analysis? If so, which areas and to what extent would you be willing to assist me?

2. How long have you been a committee member and how many successful students have you assisted?

3. Do you require a writing sample or to review my prospectus or proposal?

4. Will you sign and abide by a mentor/mentee agreement outlining the expectations between you and me?

5. What is your availability for reading and reviewing my documents and providing feedback? (Check availability in or out of class, this is important!)

6. How much assistance can I expect from you when I am stuck during researching or writing my paper?

7. What is your availability via phone, e-mail, or Skype, and in what time zone are you located?

8. How many students do you assist at one time?

9. How familiar are you with the required writing style?

10. Is there a prospective committee member you believe might be a good fit whom I should invite to join us in this endeavor? (You would ask this question if you are having a hard time finding committee members)

Obtaining knowledgeable and experienced committee members is necessary for you to be successful in your educational journey. A sample Committee Request Letter is provided in Appendix B. It is very important to learn as much about the individuals upon whom you will rely for at least 1 year—and possibly several years—depending on the type of degree program and university you attend. Asking questions is a natural way for everyone to get to know one another, and these questions will surely help break the ice and start your relationships on a solid foundation of communication and understanding, and therefore, **Keep it Simple, Scholars!**

CHAPTER 4

GETTING STARTED: CHOOSING YOUR TOPIC

Before you can begin doing much of anything with a thesis or dissertation, you need to decide on and know something about a research topic. Choosing a topic can be as easy as brushing your teeth, or as difficult as pulling your teeth! The main thing to do is determine what topic is most important to you, your future, or to individuals around you and their future. Take the time to be sure your topic aligns with the type of degree program you are following, as the topic is what drives your entire paper. The main thing is to **Keep it Simple, Scholars!**

Another way to determine a topic that is best for your degree program and personal ideals is to begin conducting research on the topic. Read the published dissertations of other students and research journal articles using keywords matching your topic. This basic research can help you determine the saturation of information regarding your topic in the event you might need to have a different perspective. If you discover little research exists about your topic, you should place most of your attention in that area as this could be the gap that could fulfill furthering the knowledge about the topic.

Some university review panels require students to provide a short prospectus outline (see Appendix C) or completed research plan (see Appendix D) about the chosen topic to obtain approval or denial and before conducting a lot of research. Some university review panels wait until the student submits a fully written proposal to deny a topic, a process of which many students disagree, but do not know about until it is too late. Check to see what your university requirements are, and follow them so that you do the least work and barriers for choosing a topic.

Try not to choose a controversial topic as this can cause individuals who review your proposal to reject the topic. Some universities provide vague parameters about topic selection; however, all university students who are conducting human subject research must obtain certain certifications and approvals prior to actually conducting a research study. That is, the Institutional Review Board (IRB) can decline a topic if it appears the topic may be too controversial, cause emotional or physical harm to people, or is too complicated for obtaining a university degree.

Finally, be sure to research a topic that will be of interest several years in the future. Just because a topic is hot now that you are starting your educational research journey does not mean it will still be a viable topic in 3 to 5 years. The most important part of beginning to research a topic is to continue to research the topic over a span of time. This will help you discover changes in research literature and focus of the topic. By the time you start your own research, the idea you had on day one of your degree program may already be complete by another researcher; thus, you will need to discover a new gap and new way to add to the knowledge of the topic through your own research.

One final thought for you as you move forward writing your thesis or dissertation: Remember this is a paper reporting factual information. Your writing needs to be free from a conversational tone. Sentences must be short, concise, and clear, with consistent statements throughout.

Congratulations on getting through the first step in your research journey—just remember—**Keep it Simple, Scholars!**

CHAPTER 5

CHAPTER 2: WHY WRITE THE LITERATURE REVIEW FIRST?

In my experience, my mentor had me conduct a literature review on my chosen topic BEFORE writing any other chapters of my proposal. One could ask why this would be a good idea, and the answer is simple: to determine the gap in the literature is a viable and necessary research path. Most people write Chapter 1 first, but find that after writing all the elemental sections, then researching the theoretical or conceptual framework, other studies related to the topic of choice already exist. If, however, one researches the topic and finds the noticeable gap in the literature, the ease of writing about the topic and relating the theories or concepts to the gap will be much easier.

Chapter 2 is the **Literature Review**, meaning that you, as the researcher, have pulled up various types of sources about your topic. These sources come from **Title Searches, Books, Articles, Research Documents, and Journals** found through Internet searches and university libraries. An important element of Chapter 2 is the **History of the Topic**, or a fully written review of the pros and cons of your topic, and overview of the research that supports your topic, and an overview of the research that does not substantiate your topic (Cone & Foster 2006).

The next section reveals the appropriate **Theories** or **Concepts** that support or do not support your topic, and why (Cone & Foster 2006). Remember, the literature findings should not only support your topic but also include some conflicting perspectives about your topic. This adds depth and a balance to your report of the literature. That is, you provide a review of relevant information that brought your topic to the moment you realized more research was necessary. There should be a clear determination regarding how the prior researcher's methods and designs led you to determine what method and design best fit conducting your study (Cone & Foster 2006). This is where you reveal the **Gap in the Literature**! At most universities, the gap in the literature is one of the most important parts of your paper—because this is the missing information that inspires you to conduct the research study!

Of course, you would then follow up with a **Conclusion** and **Summary** about the literature review. Knowing how your topic came into being, how it developed over a span of time, and that the topic is now at a point wherein a new direction of research can add to the knowledge of the topic is important to the next generation of researchers!

Therefore, you can now understand better why the review of the literature should be the first chapter written. With the theories or concepts researched, reviewed, and reported, you, as the researcher, can now direct your reader to the important gap necessitating the conduction of your research. That is, you must be sure to write about what is now missing from the implications and conclusions or strengths and weaknesses revealed in the review of other research findings—what it is that you will do in your research project that will fill the missing gap in the literature. Think about the various methods and designs used by prior researchers. If the majority of prior studies used one method over another, perhaps a study using a different method might be beneficial!

In Chapter 2, there should be a **logical flow** of information guiding the reader to information about the gap in the literature (Cone & Foster, 2006). The literature review should flow as logically as a life story--when you were born, your teen years, your first job, and marriage—because that is exactly what a literature review is—the life story (history) of your topic!

Understanding the logical flow, as if you were writing a recipe, is beneficial for this process! Writing the literature review first will make writing and linking your gap in the literature in Chapters 1 and 3. Thus, with practicing writing in logical order will make your journey so much easier, and give you the guidance you need to create a sound research project!

<u>Remember, Keep it Simple, Scholars!</u>

CHAPTER 6

BASIC ELEMENTS OF CHAPTER 1: THE INTRODUCTION TO THE STUDY

This chapter is going to be an overview of the most basic elements needed to complete Chapter 1 and are based on information provided by Cone and Foster (2006), Yin (2014), and Creswell (2013), whom most universities ask students NOT to cite, but whose information is very clear and helpful. Again, these headings are not all encompassing, and some universities may have different heading levels. However, Chapter 1 should include, at the very least, the information that follows in this section.

The **Background of the Problem** is essential for introducing the topic about which you will be researching and writing. This is not a literature review, per se, but a quick introduction to the issue under study. This is a very basic review of the current state of the topic, whom the primary theorists are in the realm of your topic, and where implications of not conducting the study should appear. Again, this is why writing Chapter 2 first is important because this section is a summary of your background of the topic from your literature review. As a scholarly topic, you should not interject how you feel about the topic, state only facts throughout this document. Start with the facts about the background of the topic by answering questions related to your topic covering the four Ws and the H (Yin, 2014): What, where, when, why, and how. What is the problem and why is it an interest? Where is this important? When and why did the topic become important? Whom does your problem affect? Who will use the information and benefit from your conducting the research? What prior research findings exist to help you investigate or address the problem? How will the proposed research extend or refine the existing knowledge in the area under study?

After writing about the overall background of the topic, provide a **Statement of the Problem**. First, offer a general statement of the problem (the big picture/macro) then scale down to the specific problem (the miniscule issue/micro). You can use a declarative statement, such as "It is not known if and to what degree or extent..." or "It is not known how or why..." or "While the literature indicated _____it is unknown if or to what extent..." Follow up with how your study findings will contribute to making the problem better, and for whom. Be sure to consistently restate and repeat your problem statement throughout the paper.

When stating how your study findings will contribute to solving the problem you will need to add that the **Purpose of the Study** is TO DO something **about the problem** (thus restating the problem). Include a clear definition of the research method (qualitative, quantitative, or mixed) and the design (correlational, quasi-experimental, or descriptive; or case study or phenomenology), population affected, and geographical location. Examples of the beginning of purpose statements suggested by Cone and Foster (2006) include:

Quantitative: The purpose of this quantitative (add the type of design you will be doing) research is to _____.

Qualitative: The purpose of this qualitative (add the type of design you will be doing) study is to understand the phenomenon under study to _____.

You can obtain citations and references regarding the best way to begin a purpose statement from many foundational researchers. Be sure to consistently restate and repeat your purpose statement throughout the paper. Read and research the best way for you to state succinctly and clearly the purpose for your research--that this is the very statement that reveals the significance of conducting your entire study!

Identifying the **Significance of the Problem** includes describing the implications of the potential results of the study based on the problem statement, research questions, and/or hypotheses, phenomenon under study. The focus of this section is to inform the reader how the research fits within and will contribute to the current body literature or research and reveal potential practical applications from the findings to improve conditions or increase knowledge for the population, community, or society affected by the problem.

An explanation of the **Rationale or Nature of the Study** expands on the information regarding the sample population. The elements of this section include how many people to select for the study, the method and design for the study, instrumentation (triangulation and validation methods may be briefly noted here), and very brief overview of the data collection process (something that will be written in detail in Chapter 3). Part of this process is to provide a short description of the selected **Research Method and Design Appropriateness**, leading back to the description of the research focus.

The focus of the research should match and align with the design for the **Research Question(s) (RQ)**, based on the problem statement, and aligned with the type of research method chosen (Creswell, 2009). If one is conducting a qualitative study, there should be one research question, and possibly one or two sub-questions. If one is conducting a quantitative study, at least one research question must be paired with a **Hypothesis**, or actually a set of hypotheses: the alternative hypothesis (**H1^a**) and the null hypothesis (**H1^0**) (Creswell, 2009)

A **Conceptual Framework or Theoretical Framework** should provide a direct connection to the conceptual or theoretical framework that will effectively guide the study and allow situation of the findings to be within a greater context (Creswell, 2009; Yin, 2014). One should start by introducing the primary theorists and describing how their theories advanced the literature about your topic. The most prevalent theories include Bandura's (1986) Social Cognitive Theory, Maslow's (1954) Hierarchy of Needs, Knowles (1980) Adult Learning Theory but others are also important to the expansion of scholarly research. You will want to include information about how your specific research relates to the theories presented, and how the information will help you in your quest to fill the gap in the literature. Establishing a conceptual or theoretical framework reveals the significance of conducting your study.

Readers might require assistance with the **Definition of Terms** used in your research. Write a brief statement about the use of the term, for example, some people use African American and Black interchangeably—this would be important to reveal, as it may seem inconsistent to some readers. Support each definition with a citation from a peer-reviewed and primary source. Dictionaries, thesauri, Wikipedia, and encyclopedias are NOT scholarly nor peer-reviewed sources for citations.

Assumptions are a self-evident truth about the information gathered in the study (Cone & Foster, 2006). State the assumptions for the study as methodological, theoretical, or topic-specific. One assumption could be that survey participants will be honest to the best of their ability when providing their answers. You could add an assumption that the study will be an accurate representation of the current situation related to the topic. Investigate to determine if any other assumptions exist and report them as necessary. Be sure provide an explanation to support your assumptions.

The **Scope** of the study is where you will identify the exact factors concerning your study. For example, if you were studying the effects of extreme temperatures on animals, perhaps the specific scope would be studying dogs and cats living outside in very hot or frigid temperatures. The scope is the narrow and specific parameters of the study factors.

There is a difference between the **Limitations** and **Delimitations** in your study. Just as the word infers, a limitation is something out of your control; something you cannot make or stop happening. Limiting issues could be the number of people available for a sample population, a geographic location, people's availability, weather, obtaining approvals, and so on. A delimitation is something you have control over as the creator of this research project; thus, the same things that could be a limitation, could affect what you choose to include or exclude from the study paradigm. A delimiting factor could be your study questions, selection of your method and design, geographic location, timeline for conducting the study, and so forth.

Of course, you would then follow up with a Conclusion and Summary about the content of Chapter 1. Add a short synopsis of each elemental heading and the importance to conducting the study. Provide an overview of what to expect for the remainder of the study. Finish the chapter by segueing to Chapter 2, and **Keep it Simple, Scholars!**

CHAPTER 7

THE "RECIPE"
CHAPTER 3: METHOD

According to the majority of my clients over a span of 6 years, Chapter 3 is the most difficult chapter to write. I must disagree—and I think you will, too! Once you read this chapter, you will discover that Chapter 3 is similar to writing a recipe: you list all the ingredients in the necessary order for inclusion in the recipe, but add very specific information about why each ingredient is important.

For this chapter, there is a lot of information to cover and some can be confusing. As a helpful guide, I have inserted a Dissertation Content Example to help guide you to formatting a quality paper (see Appendix E). The document includes the usual basic elements expected in a dissertation and in this chapter; however, some universities have a set template in which students can write that may not include any or all of these elements. Appendix F is a list of possible documents that may be required for obtaining permissions and IRB approvals. Always ask your mentor for guidance if you are unsure of what elemental headings are required for your specific university. Remember to **Keep it Simple, Scholar**s!

Research Method and Design Appropriateness. There are two types of research methods: qualitative and quantitative. In qualitative research, the investigator uses words to describe and disseminate the study information (Yin, 2014). In quantitative research, the investigator uses numbers to describe and disseminate the study information (Creswell, 2006). You should research these methods thoroughly, and remember to select the best the method needed to find the data you desire. A good researcher will try to gather as much information as possible to determine the proper method needed for the study and be able to elaborate on why the selected method is the correct one for researching the topic.

The design and method for a study must align. Qualitative designs include **Grounded Theory, ethnography, historical, case study, and phenomenology** (Yin, 2014). An additional qualitative study design is Participatory Action Research (Fals-Borda, 1987). Grounded theory is the most difficult design because the purpose is to create new theory. Ethnography is appropriate for investigating cultural issues; the researcher must be immersed in the culture and interact directly with participants.

The historical method requires the investigation of a topic from a historical perspective and relating the information to the present or future. A case study involves investigating a topic pertaining to groups of people through observation and interaction with participants. Phenomenology requires describing participant's experiences as they are lived—so that one can say they have "walked in the participant's shoes." Proper research in this area requires rationalization for using the specified design. **Participatory Action Research** is a design used by students in social services, psychosociology, community outreach and development, public health, and similar programs. The focus of this type of research is that the "action must be done 'with' people and not 'on' or 'for' people," (Fals-Borda, 1987). Regardless of the design, be sure to select the most appropriate one for your study requirements.

Research Questions and **Sub-questions (qualitative) or Hypotheses (quantitative).** Depending on the method and design selected for your research, you will need to develop research questions (RQs). Some qualitative methods require sub-questions (SQs) to help scale the scope of the study further (Yin, 2014). Quantitative RQs require a pair of hypotheses (Creswell, 2006). First, list the alternate hypothesis ($H1^a$); that is, this is the hypothesis that states the answer to the RQ will be true. Then list the null hypothesis ($H1^0$), which is the hypothesis that states the answer is not true. The number of RQs you include in your study may vary, but remember the acronym **KISS—Keep it Simple Scholars!** Try to keep the dissertation short—write your book when you are Master or Dr. YOU!

Population and Sample. Just as there are different methods and designs in research, the same follows with determining the sample population for one's research. A *population* is a small number of individuals who represent the whole group of the population. For

25

example, if there are 500 schools and each has a librarian, the population is 500 librarians. However, a *sample* of that population might only be from five to 20 individuals for a qualitative study (Yin, 2014), or 100 individuals for a quantitative study (Creswell, 2009). A review of the various notable qualitative and quantitative researchers at the time of your study is necessary to ensure you choose the correct number of participants for your study.

Sampling Technique. The various methods of research also have specific types of sampling techniques for recruiting participants. The two most prevalent in academic research are purposive sampling and random sampling. Generally, researchers use purposive sampling for qualitative studies and random sampling for quantitative studies (Creswell, 2006; Yin, 2014). However, you should research the best method to suit the method and design of your study.

Geographic Location. Interestingly, a geographic location is the area where the research will take place. Some researchers find a sample population within a specific radius of where they live; others might use a particular region of a country. Some research involves a worldwide sample population; thus, the geographic location is global. Be sure the geographic location best fits the needs for the study.

Informed Consent. One of the most important parts of conducting ethical research is to provide informed consent to the individuals who are participating. Conducting research involves many factors that participants must know so they make the best decision for themselves. Most universities require researchers to take courses to learn the various requirements of informed consent, such as the Collaborative Institutional Training Initiative (CITI, 2016) course, and review the Department of Health and Human Services (DHHS, 2016) policy, specifically 45 CFR 46. The basics are that participants know the topic of the study, the benefits, or risks of participating, if they will be audio or video recorded, options to withdraw from the study (see Appendix G for an example of a Participant Withdrawal form). Participants must also be aware of all the research processes and understand the methods of dissemination of the information.

Confidentiality. Part of the informed consent process includes the assurance of confidentiality and anonymity of ALL participants (CITI, 2016; DHHS, 2016). Be sure you understand that ALL participants includes organizations from whom you might recruit participants or ask to use protected data, places where you might interview participants, and other researchers whose documents you may ask to use in your research. As a researcher, not only is it your responsibility to ensure everyone who participates in your study is anonymous but also to secure all the data, so that the collection of any personally identifiable information is also confidential; that only you, as the researcher, will have access to that information. There usually is a time limit associated with retaining research documents; check your specific university standards and abide by them.

Ethical Considerations. One of the main ethical considerations, as previously mentioned, is the protection of your study participants through informed consent and assurance of confidentiality (CITI,

2016; DHHS, 2016). Be aware, however, that study participants not only include the individuals who participate in your data collection process but also any organizations from whose leaders you obtain permissions to conduct your study—to use a room in a building, to use internal or external e-mail or other communication methods, even archived data should be protected.

A second very important ethical consideration is the remuneration of study participants. This issue has become the subject of increasing debate among university leaders, students, and IRB. Although the DHHS (2016) provides rules and regulations in 45 CFR 46 for human subjects as participants in educational research, the definition of coercion is not clear. However, the DHHS (2016) 45 CFR 46 states that individuals must participate voluntarily not because they may or may not receive a benefit from participation. An exception might be to offer a prepaid gas card to help offset the cost of travel for participants who may travel more than 10 miles to attend a face-to-face interview. Some university IRBs may allow some minimal gift as a thank you; however, it would be best to do two things. First, ask for clarification from your university IRB liaison about offering participation gifts. Second, mention the thank you gift in your proposal but be sure that participants do not find out about the gift until after they have signed the informed consent, or at the conclusion of the interview. If the IRB approves the gift, withholding information about the gift is the best choice to indicate the reasons for participation are genuinely on inclusion in the research and not on receiving a gift.

IRB Clarification. Do you KNOW when your research study should be EXEMPT vs. NON-EXEMPT?

Exempt means there is little risk and that one is NOT researching a protected class. Therefore, full IRB approval is not required.

Non-Exempt means risk is medium to high, one is researching a protected class, or the research process indicates some chance of some harm to participants is apparent. Therefore, full IRB approval is required.

Instrumentation. Data collection requires some type of data collection instrument. For qualitative data, the researcher IS the instrument (Yin, 2014). That is, the researcher develops a set of questions to ask participants and collects each individual's responses. Quantitative data are usually collected by conducting surveys (Creswell, 2009). Some researchers create surveys or request permission to use existing surveys from previously conducted and validated studies.

Appropriateness for Instrumentation for this Study. Following the guidelines noted above, the researcher must be able to substantiate the selection of the type of data collection instrument used for the study. One would not use a survey with Likert-type scale scores for a qualitative study. One would not do well to use open-ended questions for a quantitative study. Be sure ready to explain how and why the chosen instrument will be helpful for collecting the right type of data for your study.

Permissions needed to use Instrumentation. Obtaining permission to use an existing survey or set of questions can sometimes be a very difficult process. Unless stated clearly in writing that a particular data collection instrument can be used freely, you must determine copyright ownership and ask permission to use the document. Additionally, if your particular study parameters require modification of an existing data collection instrument, be sure to ask for permission to modify the document. Explain to the copyright holder what you wish to change and why it is beneficial for your study need to do so.

Pilot Study or Field Test? This is a gray area for most academic research. You should check with your university to determine which type of testing must occur when you create a new qualitative questionnaire or quantitative survey instrument for data collection.

Pilot Study. A pilot study involves the actual administration of a proposed survey or questionnaire for collecting topic-specific data (Esposito, 2010). A pilot study involves having from two to four people who meet the participation criterion you set for your quantitative study participate in a trial study. This small-scale study is helpful to you in several ways. First, you have an opportunity to ask your questions or have participants complete the survey and you obtain data.

From that data, you can tell if you are collecting THE data you need to answer your RQs. Additionally, you have an opportunity to obtain feedback from the participants about the questions. Did the

30

participants understand the questions? Is there another way to ask your questions that is clearer? Is the question truly relevant to the research? Once you find out this information, you can update the questions for use in the main study.

Field Test. A field test requires assistance from subject matter experts (SMEs) knowledgeable in your topic of study. The SMEs can be professors, researchers, program managers, or sponsors for your researcher (Esposito, 2010). What the SME is looking for is the substance of your questions: Will the participants understand your questions? Are the questions clear, or do they need revising for clarity? Are the questions relevant to the topic of research? Does the SME believe the questions will elicit the responses necessary to answer the overarching RQ/SQ? You can have the SME complete a Field Test Feedback form (see Appendix H) for proof your interview questions were reviewed and approved by topic expert.

Remember that you should not have your pilot study or field test participants participate in the main study, nor should you use the findings from the testing process in the final study results. For clarity; however, you should report what occurred during the pilot study or field test in a separate portion in Chapter 4. List the information under a specific heading for the results of the pilot study or field test and specify the exclusion of the participants from the main study. These are the fundamental purposes of conducting a pilot study or field test, and apply to all types of research studies (Leon, Davis, & Kraemer, 2010).

Validity and Reliability. Inclusion of each of these elements is dependent on your research method and design, and your instrumentation. For quantitative studies, the validity is the extent to which a test measures what it is supposed to measure. Reliability is the degree to which a test consistently measures whatever it measures (Creswell, 2009).

Credibility, Transferability, Dependability, & Confirmability. According to Lincoln and Guba (1985) these elements are necessary for a qualitative study:

a) Credibility is the congruency of the findings with reality.

b) Transferability is the generalizability of the study and extent to which the findings of one study are applicable to another study.

c) Dependability means the same results would occur if the study were repeated.

d) Confirmability is a way to ensure as far as possible that the work's findings are the result of the experiences and ideas of the informants and there is no researcher bias.

Triangulation. Yin (2009) revealed six methods of data collection that help with triangulation: Documentation, archived records, interviews, direct observation, participant observation, and artifacts. Many documents are easily accessible to the public on the Internet or through libraries. However, some data requires permission to access, including participant observations and interviews. As the researcher, you must determine which types of data best fits your specific study to meet university, IRB, and CITI requirements.

Bracketing and Epoché. Bracketing involves setting aside one's preconceptions in all aspects of conducting the research (Creswell, 2009). The researcher must eliminate all bias or understanding of the concept and try to understand the phenomenon from the perspective provided by the data collected (Moustakas, 1994). Epoché is the theoretical moment where the researcher begins to ignore and suspend all personal judgments about the topic and conduct the research from the perspective of learning something new and fresh— as if never having previous knowledge of the topic (Moustakas, 1994).

Data Collection. This part of your research should be the most exciting of all! You obtained IRB approval to conduct your study and can recruit your participants! Having a letter of recruitment or a flyer is extremely important because this document is the introduction to your study (see Appendix H). Follow the plan you outlined for qualitative or quantitative methods. If you conducted a pilot study, use the same format for the main portion of your study.

Data Analysis. Several data analysis choices are available, depending on your research method and design. For quantitative studies, most researchers use Statistical Package for the Social Sciences™ (SPSS) software or Atlas.ti™; however, there are other programs available. Check to see which is best for the type of study you are conducting. Qualitative researchers have several options for data analysis.

First, if interviews were audio tape recorded, transcribing the recordings personally can add to the depth and richness of the manual data analysis process, because you were there asking the questions, you heard the responses, and now you are hearing the same information a second time. This process provides you a higher rate of accuracy of verbatim transcripts. The greatest benefit is the recollection of information and clarity of understanding that can come from transcribing, coding, and developing themes from your own data collection process. That is, get out a pen and some paper; perhaps use Microsoft Excel to list your data in groups and codes. Considering the researchers is present and involved during the interview process, it only makes sense to manually and personally analyze the data for a more rich, in-depth report of the results, implications, and conclusions.

Second, some researchers hire a transcriptionist to provide Word copies of each interview, then manually code the data. Finally, some researchers take the transcribed data and use NVivo™, MAXQA™, or Atlas.ti™ software to assist with coding and creating themes.

Member Checking. Member checking is a valuable tool for ensuring participant data accurately represents the statements and perceptions of participants (Lincoln & Guba, 1985). Many researchers conduct member checking after transcribing the interviews to help improve the accuracy, credibility, validity, and transferability (internal validity) of the information. Lincoln and Guba (1985) revealed various types of member checking, such as narrative accuracy checks, interpretive validity, descriptive validity, theoretical validity, and evaluative validity. The type of member checking you select should match the study design; which in turn will help provide authenticity of the data.

Of course, you would then follow up with a Conclusion and Summary about the content of Chapter 3. Add a short synopsis of each elemental heading and the importance of the method and design for the study. Provide an overview of what to expect for the remainder of the study with by segueing to Chapters 4 and 5—and **<u>Keep it Simple, Scholars!</u>**

CHAPTER 8

THE FINISHING TOUCH: CHAPTER 4: FINDINGS
&
CHAPTER 5: CONCLUSIONS, IMPLICATIONS, &
RECOMMENDATIONS FOR FURTHER RESEARCH

The purpose of Chapter 4 is to present the results, findings, and conclusions from conducting the data analysis. This chapter is reserved for reporting all the factual data without implication, speculation, assessment, evaluation, or interpretation. The interpretation of the study results are the focus of Chapter 5.

Chapter 4: Findings

Begin Chapter 4 by being sure to write in the past tense (not passive voice) with a short overview of the purpose of the study and follow with expected content. Represent the data using clearly marked headings for qualitative analysis results, or in the form of charts, graphs, tables, or statistics. Present the information and data in the same presentation order as the research questions and/or hypotheses.

The **Results** from your study are unique; thus, it is difficult to offer direction for the formatting of this chapter. Everything

36

reported in Chapter 4 is going to be about the **Findings**, as the researcher, from the data collected in your study. The logical flow of your report of the findings will also depend upon your method (qualitative or quantitative) and design (case study or correlational). However, depending on what is most appropriate for your study type, you can organize the data by research question, chronology of variables, themes, and patterns.

Of great importance is to determine whether it is appropriate to include citations in Chapter 4. Generally, Chapter 4 should only be a report of what you found from conducting your study. In previous chapters, you informed your reader when, where, why, how, and from whom you determined the plan for your data collection process in alignment with your chosen method and design. In Chapter 4, you only need report that you followed the plan defined in Chapter 3 followed by revealing what you discovered in the analysis of that data. Complete the chapter with a conclusion, summary, and segue to Chapter 5.

Chapter 5: Conclusion, Implications, & Recommendations for Further Research

Chapter 5 is the final and most important chapter of a thesis or dissertation. The focus of the chapter is to provide a summative report of the findings from conducting the study; thus, an overview of the entire study beginning with a refreshing introduction about the problem and purpose for the study, reiteration of the research questions and/or hypotheses, and findings from the research study.

Do not report new data or add new citations in this chapter; draw from the information and literature from your earlier research. First, offer a **Review of the Problem**, restate why the research was important and to whom. Provide a **Summary of the Literature** wherein you indicate literature that supports the findings, and literature that does not support the findings, and a short synopsis of why each is important.

Explain the process of **Conducting the Research**. You could state if any barriers or limitations you expected did or did not occur. You could also update your assumptions if you assumed correctly or incorrectly, what would happen during the data collection process.

Next, you should provide a **Review of the Findings** in the same order as provided in Chapter 4. Some universities want the review of the findings in the same order and format as listed in Chapter 4. Double-check your university requirements in this regard.

When reporting the **Conclusions from the Findings**, emphasize the most important points one should note about the information. Do so for each theme or important finding. For the **Implications**, answer the questions, "What does this mean for you [the reader]?" of "How are the findings applicable to changing/helping the situation [in some industry]?"

This section of Chapter 5, **Recommendations for Future Research**, is where you, the researcher and author, will guide your reader to a gap in the topic or findings you discovered after conducting your research! For example, perhaps you conducted a qualitative study and identified five overarching themes. However, something stated by one participant was something you were unable to report on, and indicates a new direction for research about your topic—you should note that for further research. You could state future researcher could acquire different results using a quantitative method and design to discover something new about the topic, uncaptured using a qualitative method. Finally, provide a comprehensive Conclusion and Summary that reviews the entire study, from Chapter 1 thorough Chapter 5, and ends with a distinctive and interesting statement about further research about the topic.

When you reach this point in your journey **YOU ARE ALMOST DONE!** Your paper is in front of the Dean for final approval—look back on your use of this book. Were you able to **keep it simple**— and now that you ARE a **scholar**—do you realize you have made it to the end of your degree program and are about to be a published author?

Next might be your oral defense. Work with your mentor to produce a high-quality presentation of your dissertation. If you use Microsoft Power Point, make a master copy with notes at the bottom of each slide to help you stay on track if a conversation ensues during your presentation! Provide your committee a copy without notes. Once you are done, and you pass, your committee will address you as Master or Doctor **YOU** for the first time! CONGRATULATIONS!

CHAPTER 9

WRITE LIKE A SCHOLAR: BASIC EDITING ISSUES

Now that you have an idea of how to put your dissertation or thesis together, you can learn what errors to look for and learn how to fix many of these editorial issues yourself. The idea behind providing scholars with this information is to help offset the extreme expense for editing assistance. Thus, if you choose to use this guide to help you write your dissertation or thesis from the beginning stages, you should have very few editorial issues—meaning you should not have to pay an exorbitant amount of money for an editor to review your paper for university submission and approvals. This is one way to **Keep it Simple, Scholars!**

One of my greatest peeves about the editing industry is that university students are ripped off by folks who say they are editors, when they truly only use the features of Word and possibly some editorial software programs to find errors. Some people can proofread and find a few misspellings or unfinished sentences; however, these individuals do not have the training, certification, or experience in what the university reviewers are looking for in a scholarly paper. These individuals have only one thing in mind, and that is to transfer money from your wallet to their wallet—and charge much more money to provide students with a paper that is still unacceptable for conducting research or publication.

The main reason for this book is to provide university scholars with basic tools to write and edit their paper to the very best of their ability before having to hire a dissertation coach or editor. In this light, the fee for professional editing should be more manageable, and the final product should take less time to edit, revise, and format for submission.

The remainder of this chapter includes various examples of the most common and notable errors from the reviews and revisions of real doctoral dissertation proposals, with the permission of the authors. An explanation or suggested revision follows each error. These examples may help you learn to recognize your own errors in your paper, and give you an opportunity to make the corrections yourself; thus, lessening the time a professional editor would need to edit your paper.

Following are terms one might hear or read from individuals who assist them with the thesis or dissertation writing process. Become familiar with these terms, and practice reviewing your own paper for instances of these extremely common grammatical errors and correct the statements accordingly. This will be the first step in saving time and money hiring outside editorial assistance—and help make YOU a better, more aware, scholarly writer!

Abbreviations and Acronyms. Use as few acronyms and abbreviations as possible. Each of the writing style manuals list abbreviations and acronyms as an issue with clarity and continuity of thought for the reader. Generally, it is better to write out a term than to use an acronym, especially if the acronym may be confused with one that is the actual name of an organization. For example, DEA could be the Drug Enforcement Agency or Department of Environmental Advocacy. However, if a reviewer were to see this in a paper, the first thing that would come to mind is the Drug Enforcement Agency. Even if you were to list this in the definition of terms in Chapter 1, many folks would probably become confused about the organization. If in doubt, spell it out!

For cities, states, and countries, one should write out the names fully. Some universities allow the abbreviation for the United States as U. S. For consistency, spelling out the names of geographic locations adds to the ease of read and clarity in the paper.

Affect versus Effect and Substituting Impact. Affect is a verb meaning to influence something: "John's cut in salary will ***affect*** our ability to go on vacation this year." Effect is a noun describing a result: "John's cut in salary is the ***effect*** of revenue loss by the company." Several universities allow the substitution of the word impact for both affect and effect; however, the word impact is generally associated more with the collision of two objects: "I saw the cars break apart on ***impact***."

So, if we take the two sentences above and substitute impact for affect and effect:

- "John's cut in salary will affect our ability to go on vacation this year."

- "John's cut in salary will impact our ability to go on vacation this year."

- "John's cut in salary is the effect of revenue loss by the company."

- "John's cut in salary is the impact of revenue loss by the company."

The choice of word use is up to the student author; however, part of writing a thesis or dissertation is to learn about all the aspects of writing, including using the proper words in the correct context.

Anthropomorphism. The definition of anthropomorphism is the act of giving the characteristics of humans to an animal, a god, or an inanimate thing (Merriam-Webster's Collegiate Dictionary, 20014). The study, method, design, literature review, data analysis process or software, findings, and so forth are not human; therefore, they cannot see, describe, examine, explain, define, determine, analyze, or do any other action requiring human thought, touch, vision, verbiage, smell, or taste. Anthropomorphism can also be confused with **personification**, which is similar to anthropomorphism in that one projects an inanimate object or true object, such as a dog, as having human qualities: The dog kept asking for a bone, wherein the dog cannot speak.

- *An example of anthropomorphism:* <u>The study will use</u> a qualitative methodology and a phenomenological design using Moustakas' modified van Kaam analysis to develop clusters of meaning.

- *An example of writing to remove anthropomorphism:* Conducting this study required using a qualitative method and a phenomenological design and Moustakas' modified van Kaam analysis to develop clusters of meaning.

Appendixes: Be sure that if you use appendixes for your paper that you list them in the EXACT order in which they appear first in the paper. To be clear: If you state you obtained signed permission to use the local library on page 1, that document should be listed as Appendix A, and also be listed first in the list of appendixes in the back of the document, which usually follows the list of references. With each successive mention of a new appendix, give the correct label (Appendix B, C, and D) and place in the back matter as noted.

Expletives. In scholarly writing, *there is, there are, there was, there were, it is, and it was,* are phrases used in place of naming the subject. These words usually appear at the beginning of a sentence.

As you can see from the examples below, moving the subject to the beginning of the sentence makes the statement clear and concise.

- There are five dogs running throughout the neighborhood.

- Five dogs are running throughout the neighborhood.

Font. University guidelines provide students with the formatting requirements for the thesis or dissertation. Be sure to double-check your paper for consistent font size and style. When you copy and paste from other saved research documents, the font size and style may not be the same or might change, if your settings are different or you do not choose to use the current font formatting.

Formatting. Formatting is an area noted where many theses and dissertations do not meet the requirements for publication according to many university reviewers. Unless one is a master of Word and understands all the nuances of the formatting process, students can choose to do several things to polish their papers for submission. The student could investigate web-based tutorials about how to format a paper in Word, ask a friend who knows how to format in Word, or hire an editor to format the paper according to university requirements for approvals and publication.

Levels of Headings. Depending on the writing style your university requires, there should be several levels of headings in your paper. The headers indicate the level of importance of each topic; thus, if a topic has sub-topics, the levels of headings change to indicate the relationship of the sub-topic information to the main topic. Several universities require as few as three levels of headings, and others require up to five levels of headings. Be sure to meet these levels of headings as much as possible—and be sure to format the headings accurately, for logical flow, and ease of read.

Numbers. Numbers are one of the most difficult areas of writing protocols for most people to grasp. This information should help you understand better how to use numbers—but again—this depends on the style of writing the university requires. Both APA and MLA use the following information. The CMS style of writing has very few instances where one would use ordinal numbers.

The best way to understand the rules about using numbers is that with the exception of statistical use and units of time, (e.g., seconds, minutes, hours, days, months, years, decades, or millennia), use ordinal numbers. The two exceptions to this rule are when beginning a sentence or approximations of time:

- The boys earned their degrees in 4 years.

- The boys will earn their degrees in about four years.

- Four years ago, the boys earned their degrees.

For other uses of numbers, the rule is to write out in words the numbers one through nine, and use ordinal numbers for 10 and above.

Opinion. Everyone has an opinion; however, your thesis or dissertation is not where you want to include personal opinions about your topic. Writing about research in a scholarly tone requires one to write only facts. Reporting of facts must come from the review of the literature or from reporting the findings from the research.

Paragraphs: A paragraph is a block of information related to a topic and contains at least three sentences. Several universities provide an outline for students called the MEAL plan. The MEAL plan stands for (a) Main idea, (b) Evidence, (c) Analysis, and (d) Link back to main topic. Remember to write a transition sentence to move the topic forward to the next paragraph. Several outlines and further descriptions of the MEAL plan are available on the Internet and university websites. Follow the plan, and write clear, concise, and informative paragraphs!

Parentheses. Overuse of parentheses in a thesis or dissertation is a detriment to clear and concise writing. Use parentheses to set off structurally independent elements; to enclose citation years in text or to set parenthetical citations; introduce an abbreviation or acronym; for seriation of items in a series in a sentence; and for mathematical or statistical information.

Participants. When writing a thesis or dissertation, choose one term to identify the individuals involved in your research. Participants are the most widely used term. Other researchers may use respondents or interviewees, which are not clear about the involvement in your study. Someone can respond to your invitation to participate in the study, but decline afterward. Individuals can respond and be an interviewee—making the person a participant.

Passive Voice. Interestingly, we speak and think passively; that is, as we learn to speak as children, other people around us speak in passive voice. Why? Because it is easy, and it is just the natural way for people to think and speak. In general, there is nothing wrong with speaking or writing using passive voice; however, when it comes to academic and scholarly writing, you must change the way you express the facts and information provided from your research. Many of these passive phrases are marked with squiggly lines and with the term *passive voice* in Word using the Spelling & Grammar tab.

There are cues editors look for in scholarly writing, and this list is only a few of the most common cues that I look for when editing a scholarly theses or dissertation. First, I look for specific verbs ending in "__ed__" preceded by the following *linking verbs*, which are verbs that imply action but do nothing (Lester & Beason, 2013): is, are, be, being, was, were, had, has, have, to be, have been, had been, could have, would have, will be, to be.

- *Example of incorrect writing with passive voice*: A qualitative phenomenological process **will be used** to seek the understanding of the individual perspectives of successful small business owners during recession through in-depth interviews.

- *Example of correct writing with active past tense*: The conduction of this study **required using** a qualitative phenomenological process to obtain an understanding of the individual perspectives of successful small business owners during economic recessions through semi-structured, in-depth interviews.

Past Tense. This is sometimes confused with *passive voice*, so the best way to explain this is that the subject performs the action. Using the example of Jane as the subject and walk as the verb above:

- *Example 1*: "Jane (subject) **walked** (verb in the past tense) to school before."

- *Example 2*: Passive voice would be, "**Jane** (subject) **has walked** (verb with *linking verb*) to school before."

Pronouns. Pronoun use is an area of scholarly writing that may be an issue with university reviewers. A request for the exclusion of pronouns depends on your university writing parameters and sometimes, the whim of whomever reviews your paper. References to they, them, their, he/she, his/her replace the subject or subjects (students, teachers, authors, dogs, engineers) or incorrectly define an object or objects (rocks, plants, cars).

Punctuation. Few people know when to use a colon not a semi-colon, or a semi-colon not a comma. Apostrophes are another difficult punctuation mark, defining the plural and plural possessive of people and things.

Quotation Mark Errors: Sometime a word or phrase requires emphasis—to make a discerning point clear. However, double quotation marks are an indication of quoted text. If you put words or phrases inside double quotation marks, the information MUST be a quote, properly cited, and include a page, paragraph, or some information about where one can find the direct quote. If you use quotation marks incorrectly, you could receive a charge of plagiarism. Also, remember than if you have quote within quoted text, you use single quotation marks. If you have a quote that is more than 40 words, you must use a blocked quote format. Refer to your writing style manual for more information.

Redundancy: Part of the process of writing a thesis or dissertation includes restating certain information to keep reviewers engaged in reading the paper. Unfortunately, the requirement to restate certain passages in the paper may extend the opportunity for you to repeat words and phrases—sometimes entire paragraphs—without noticing. For example, this sentence: "The informed consent includes an introduction to the *researcher* along with *researcher* contact information." Use of the term the researcher here may be accurate but revising the statement to eliminate the reference to the researcher is best: "The informed consent includes information about the research project and specific contact information, should a participant have questions or concerns." This revision takes out the redundancy and the direct referent to the researcher, but infers the participants can contact the researcher with questions!

Run-on Sentences. When writing a dissertation, there is so much information, one might want to include in the paper but trying to define where to end each sentence could be difficult for most writers because it seems like once a period is added to the end of one sentence the next sentence might be more difficult to write. The previous sentence is a run-on sentence and includes passive voice, too. These sentences, or extremely long paragraphs, are usually marked with a squiggly line in Word when using the Spelling & Grammar tab. While it might be a grammatically correct sentence, scholarly papers require writing information and ideas clearly and concisely. Following is the revised version of the first sentence, to meet short, clear, and concise writing and removing run-on sentences:

When writing a dissertation, there is too much information to include in the paper. Defining where to end each sentence could be difficult for most writers. Adding a period to the end of one sentence does not mean the next sentence will be easier to write.

Scholarly Tone. Scholarly tone is somewhat difficult to define but mainly refers to the academic formality as a scholar and learned individual. That is, the usual conversational tone with which one speaks is not appropriate for academic and scholarly writing.

A doctoral student received this feedback in a review of a dissertation:

> I think the problem is that you are talking instead of writing. You write down what you say and that causes sentence structure error or logic problems. This is a dissertation, a research study. Please write in a scholarly tone.

> Conversational writing includes using many colloquial statements:

> *Example 1*. The findings rubbed me the wrong way, versus, I disagreed with the findings.

> *Example 2*. Reviewing the literature findings revealed a hit or miss attitude from the teacher's perspectives, versus, According to the literature review findings, no consensus about teacher perspectives occurred.

> Additionally, avoid asking rhetorical questions in your paper. The only questions that should be included in your paper are the research questions. Revise any questions you might think of, such as, "The results from the study conducted by Jones (2010) invites the question: What makes leaves on trees turn green?" so they are statements of inquiry: "The results from the study conducted by Jones (2010) revealed the need to discover why the leaves on trees turn green."

Self-referral: Avoid referring to yourself as much as possible when writing your thesis or dissertation. Most universities discourage the use of *the researcher, the author, the investigator,* and *the interviewer* as this can cause the reader to pay more attention to what you plan to do, rather than the process and information about your research study. Sparingly use *I* or *me*, but only if you must do so.

Seriation (Lists). While writing a thesis or dissertation, it may be necessary to list information. A list is helpful for setting off or emphasizing information. Bulleted lists are most common because the information appears in no particular order. Short lists contained within the text require using alphabetical seriation (a), (b), (c), and usually means the information that follows might be the next group of headings for information to come, or steps in a process. Lists containing sentences should be listed using numbers, with each numbered sentence starting on a new line. Use the appropriate method as stated in your university guide or writing style manual.

Sentence Clarity. Unfortunately, the process of writing can become tedious. You might know what you want to write and formulate information in your brain; however, when you begin to type, you might omit some words. This causes unclear or unfinished sentences. Many of these sentences are marked with squiggly lines and with the term ***fragment*** in Word using the Spelling & Grammar tab. Do not be confused with the content headings that may be flagged as fragments; review all sentences for easy of read, conciseness, and clarity. Reading sentences aloud can be helpful for finding incomplete or awkwardly stated sentences. This trick helps greatly with improving clarity!

Split infinitives. Split infinitives are part of conversational speech and go unnoticed by most people. The issue in scholarly writing is the placement of the word *to* between the adverb and verb. The blue squiggly lines in Word can help with finding split infinitives; however; using the find and replace function and looking for the word *to* can help find these errors quickly. Example 1 is an example of using a split infinitive, and Example 2 is the same statement with one word moved so that the

Example 1: The findings from the research may help leaders *to better understand* why leaves on trees turn green.

Example 2: The findings from the research may help leaders *to understand better* why leaves on trees turn green.

Another issue is the word *to* followed by words ending in *ly*. For example, these terms occur often in theses and dissertations: *to effectively increase, to quickly implement,* and *to consistently progress.*

Statistical Terms. Each of the writing style manuals includes a section regarding the formatting and display of statistical terms. Be sure to double-check with the specific writing style for your university and apply the rules accordingly. If you hire an outside statistician to assist you, be sure to follow the rules consistently for both in text descriptions of statistical results, and any tables or figures placed in the paper.

Subject-Verb Agreement. Most people do not easily understand the basics of grammar. The Internet is a wonderful source of information, wherein students ought to research the various issues or obtain a source for double-checking grammar errors. Additionally, obtaining books on grammar and writing styles can be very helpful for ensuring subject-verb agreement occurs throughout the paper. The subject-verb disagreement comes from the number of the verb not matching the number of the subject (Lester & Beason, 2013).

- *Example of correct singular noun-verb agreement*. Remembering that the **verb** is the source of the action (**walk**) and the **subject** is a person or thing (**Jane**), one would say, "**Jane walks** to school on Mondays."

- *Example of incorrect singular subject-verb agreement*. One would not say, "**Jane walk** to school on Mondays."

- *Example of correct plural subject-verb agreement*. "**The boys walk** to school on Tuesdays."

- *Example of incorrect plural subject-verb agreement*. "**The boys walks** to school on Tuesdays."

Tables and Figures. According to the majority of writing style manuals, and certainly APA, MLA, and CMS styles, tables and figures should only be included in the paper to augment what appears in the text. Thus, do not write a long, drawn out report of your findings or information, then attach a table or figure with all the same information as written. Write an introduction of what the reader will see, and then allow the reader to review the table or figure.

Another issue with listing tables and figures is the placement of the tables and titles. Generally, tables are numbered and titled above the table, with a notation or legend placed below them. Figures are numbered, titled, and captioned below the figure. Tables and figures should be set on one page. If a split table is necessary, be sure to follow the formatting instructions from the appropriate writing style manual. If a table is lengthy, it may be best to set the table as an appendix and label it as such in the paper. Be sure to review the writing style manual, and the thesis or dissertation guide provided by your university, for specific rules about setting tables and figures.

Tense Errors. When writing the proposal, provide the information in active future tense; that is, what you WILL DO once approval to conduct the research occurs. In this case, writing in the future tense includes using **will be** and **is to**. After conducting the study and completing Chapters 4 and 5, revealing the results and conclusions, the first three chapters require a tense revision, mostly the change will be **was to**.

- *Example 1*: The purpose of conducting this study **is to** (future tense) discover why leaves are green.

- *Example 2.* The purpose of conducting this study **was to** (past tense) discover why leaves are green.

Those. People are NEVER *those*. When writing about people, use the subject form about whom you are referring that is, teachers, students, doctors, nurses, cab drivers, dogs, trees. When reading a paper referring to people as *those* instead of the subject, one could ask, "Those what?"

- *Example of correct statement:* "I want to walk to school with *kids* who do not take the bus on Tuesdays."

- *Example of incorrect statement:* "I want to walk to school with *those* who do not take the bus on Tuesdays."

Transitions. While it seems scholarly to use many transitional terms, use words, such as *however, therefore, moreover, furthermore, additionally*, and so on, sparingly. Here is a comprehensive, but not exhaustive list of transitional words and phrases to avoid or use sparingly:

Accordingly, additionally, afterwards, also, alternatively, although, and, besides, but, conversely, despite, embracing, encompassing, even so, eventually, extending, finally, first, further, furthermore, hence, however, in addition, initially, in conclusion, in contrast, in spite of, likewise, meanwhile, moreover, nevertheless, next, nonetheless, not withstanding, on the contrary, on the other hand, otherwise, overall, presently, previously, rather, regardless, since, subsequently, thereafter, therefore, while. (Merriam-Webster's Collegiate Dictionary, 2014)

Verbs. Throughout my review of theses and dissertations, the following verbs are overused. Try to use various words throughout your paper and be sure to use the right words, to keep your reader interested and not remembering that you used ***stated***, ***found***, and ***showed*** in your paper hundreds of times. Yes, these are the three most overused verbs for cited materials—Chapter 2 is generally rife with them after each start-of-sentence citation: "Jones (2010) stated,…" or "The findings from research conducted by Jones (2010) found or showed…" Following is an example of some verbs in past tense (that is, ending in *ed*) to use in scholarly writing:

Acknowledged; added; addressed; administered; admitted; advised; advocated; affirmed; agreed; analyzed; argued; asserted; assessed; assumed; attempted; based; believed; characterized; claimed; clarified; compared; completed; conceded; concluded; concurred, conducted; confirmed; considered; contributed; defined; demonstrated; denied; described; determined; developed; discovered; discussed; documented; emphasized; espoused; examined; exhibited; expanded; explained; explored; expressed; formulated; found; generalized; highlighted; hypothesized; identified; implied; included; indicated; inferred; interpreted; introduced; maintained; mandated; noted; observed; opined; perceived; posited; presented; promoted; proposed; proved; provided; recognized; referenced; referred; refined; related; reported; revealed; said; served; showed; specified; spoke;

stated; stressed; studied; submitted; suggested; surveyed; theorized; thought; viewed. (Merriam-Webster's Collegiate Dictionary, 2014)

Verb-Tense Agreement. There are two notable issues: *is* versus *are*, and *was* verses *were*. A singular subject (he) takes a singular verb (is), whereas a plural subject (they) takes a plural verb (are).

Singular. I was, you were, he was, she was, it was.

Plural. We were, you were, they were.

Words and Phrases to Avoid Using out of Normal Context. Aim, amongst, due to, for the reason, for the purpose of, impact, the fact that, towards, seek, and utilize. Your university reviewers may list more words to remove or change. Remember, scholarly writing is clear, concise, and consistent.

CHAPTER 10

PLAGIARISM, CITATIONS, & REFERENCES

Plagiarism. With the advent of the Internet as an easy source for gathering data, plagiarism is an increasingly and extremely hot topic in all genres of writing scrutinized now, more than ever, in academic writing. Be sure to locate and read the Student Code of Conduct and Plagiarism Policy for your specific university. It is imperative you are completely aware of the expectations of you as a student, researcher, and author. Regardless of where one obtains the information on a topic, it is important to review the rules for plagiarism. The definition of plagiarism is "the practice of taking someone else's work or ideas and passing them off as one's own" (Merriam-Webster Dictionary, 2015). Many university rules state that plagiarism is the intended or unintended use of another person's material without citing the source.

The gray area here is the term *unintended use*. Many students believe that they *don't know what they don't know*. That is, a student may inadvertently use a saying or phrase in a paper without knowing someone cited the information somewhere. The job of a great and ethical researcher is to be certain to research as much information as possible to avoid plagiarism.

Attention is increasing in the publishing world on issues of plagiarism, accidental plagiarism, and ownership of intellectual property. Anyone who uses phrases, words, tables, figures, or surveys from outside sources will find this chapter crucial, but all writers should be well versed in copyright issues: **Remember, if you didn't write it, you need to cite it!**

Citations. Be aware that you need to use PRIMARY sources for as many citations as possible. According to the APA manual (2009) secondary sources are only used sparingly "when the original work is out of print, unavailable through usual sources, or not available in English." p. 178). Secondary sources usually have this format: Jones (2012, as cited by Stevens, 2013). The requirement for using primary sources is true for MLA and CMS writing formats, too.

The best page in the APA manual is page 177. I will use this as an example because APA is used by most universities as the thesis and dissertation writing style. On page 177, a table lists every type of citation, for in text and parenthetical citations, with numbers of authors, and types of authors. This is a great visual for double-checking the accuracy of the citations as you add them to your paper. At the very bottom of page 177, there is also information about using multiple parenthetical citations—that information is extremely important, too!

The two types of citations are: in text and parenthetical. Citations can include a single source or be a list of multiple sources. The order of citations depends upon the writing and formatting style of your university, as does the specific placement. Be sure to take the time to read and become very familiar with the writing style manual. Be sure to understand the different use of the word *and* versus the ampersand (&) in your citations. Editors may not make a change to a citation, so you must ensure you listed and formatted the citations accurately.

References. Just as with the writing and formatting style requirements for citations, you must also be sure your references meet the same criteria. Additionally, as with citations, editors cannot change references. As the author and researcher, you should have a list or copy of all your references and sources, and accurately list them in the references section of your paper. Pay specific attention to the examples provided in your specific writing and formatting style resource book. A great resource finding digital object identifier (doi) numbers, available at the time of this writing, is www.crossref.org. Also be certain that website uniform resource locators (URLs) take the reviewer *directly* to the source material—not the website, but the actual page where the source material is located.

To summarize, it is important to be absolutely certain you are giving the proper credit to your sources, through accurately paraphrasing and quoting; obtaining permission or listing copyright information; and citing and listing your references. Remember that you are proving assurance that your paper is an original document, and universities are not going to differentiate between what is intentional or unintentional plagiarism. Begin writing your paper and cite passages that are not your original thoughts about your topic or research. The rule is that is someone can ask, "Who said?" you should cite the statement.

CHAPTER 11

ETHICS OF USING OUTSIDE ASSISTANCE

The subject of using outside assistance to complete the dissertation and thesis journey has been an increasingly notable subject in the past decade. Issues with cheating, plagiarism, and just plain laziness have induced university policies to become extremely strict regarding hiring statisticians, editors, dissertation coaches, writing tutors, and transcriptionists.

Many students know their weaknesses when it comes to writing, editing, data analysis, working with math and statistics, motivation, and the art of listening and typing from recordings. Some students really do need the assistance. Therefore, it is imperative to understand the ethical boundaries of using outside assistance during the writing of dissertations and theses. Please become extremely familiar with the Student Code of Conduct and rules regarding plagiarism for your university. The Student Code of Conduct outlines the parameters in which outside assistance is acceptable. Individuals who assist you are not responsible for the accuracy of your citations and references and are not accountable for a charge of plagiarism against a student.

Editing. Most editors use tracked changes in Word to indicate suggested changes, move text for logical flow, and leave comments about issues needing the student's attention in a thesis or dissertation document. Other than formatting for presentation and publication, no permanent changes are appropriate in a degree-bearing paper. Editors can assist with correcting specific formatting issues with table and figure formatting, pagination, and offer suggested revisions for proper presentation of the references and citations.

Most universities require students to sign a letter of originality or authenticity, assuring the student is the original researcher and author of the paper. By signing the letter of originality, the student provides assurance of obtaining permission to use or citing any additional information that was not an original thought. This includes all text, tables, diagrams, and other documentation in the paper.

Contrary to most university guidelines, editors and proofreaders do not offer the same services. A copyeditor does all the work of an editor, proofreader (i.e., line-item reading and editing), writing and English grammar expert (i.e., misspelled words, noun/verb agreement, tense), content specialist, formatting, and research specialist. Thus, a copyeditor will focus on reading and editing the entire document, taking the time to review the overall organization and development, grammatical, and mechanical issues of your paper. Generally, you can ask for a light, medium, or heavy edit. Most copyeditors prefer to conduct the heavy edit, which provides the most value and finds the most errors of the three editing processes.

A proofreader will read your paper and only conduct a line-by-line review. As part of this basic service, the proofreader will only offer simple corrections, such as spelling errors, misplaced modifiers, missing references and citations, capitalization, and unfinished sentences. Be sure you decide on which type of services you need and expect.

When working with an editor, previous tracked changes and comments should not exist in the document. Correct all revisions from your committee members prior to editing. Update and revise only one version of the document. Working on a version of the paper at home on your computer while the editor is working on your paper can create errors and mistakes. Trying to merge the two papers can truly make a mess, wasting time and effort for everyone.

Dissertation Coaches and Writing Tutors. Similar to the requirements for editors, writing tutors and dissertation coaches must also use tracked changes in Word to indicate suggested changes or revisions to a student's paper. The idea for obtaining a tutor or coach is to have an expert in the dissertation writing and development process assist a student with outlining, writing, understanding, and completing the dissertation process. However, this does not include the tutor or coach researching or writing content for the student; rather, the tutor and dissertation coach reviews the student's work, and offer revisions for clarity, content, flow, and understanding, and encouragement to continue with the educational journey when motivation declines or frustrating barriers to success arise.

Dissertation Coach. The role of a dissertation coach can vary, depending on where you are in your dissertation journey. If you are just starting to write your prospectus or proposal, a dissertation coach can help you refine your topic, create and refine a problem and purpose statement, and coach you through conducting a review of literature and learning to synthesize relevant findings for your topic.

After defining the foundation of your research, the dissertation coach can help you develop your research questions and hypotheses, based on if your study requires a quantitative or qualitative methodology. A dissertation coach will also help you learn how to store and manage your data, such as making sure to back up your data to several external drives, the Cloud, or other retrievable means, in the event of computer failure or data loss. Finally, a dissertation coach can guide you through analyzing and organizing your data, and organizing your conclusions and recommendations.

Writing Tutor. A writing tutor works one-on-one with students to address specific writing issues the student may have while writing the paper. For example, a writing tutor helps students learn to recognize and correct grammatical, spelling, and punctuation issues, and fact checking of citations and references.

Transcriptionists. Transcriptionists may type a verbatim report of any audio recorded or videotaped interviews. The clear word here is *verbatim*; no matter what was said during the entire interview, each word must be accurately transcribed as stated. If words are changed or omitted, reporting of the research findings could be incorrect.

Additionally, a transcriptionist should not try to conduct any data analysis of the transcripts. Only the researcher should try to determine what information is significant from the transcribed data. Because of the difficulty in proving the abilities to transcribe data, you should ask for personal references, people you can speak with to hear about that person's experience with using the transcriptionist's services.

Statisticians. Statisticians are also ethically accountable for assuring the student working on a degree-bearing paper completes the data analysis and conducts the data reporting in the theses or dissertation. The statistician's role is to review the information provided by the student for accuracy and clarity, in accordance with statistical reporting. If changes are necessary, the statistician should coach and guide the student through the process of making corrections, and complete final reviews. The creation of tables, figures, and other types of visual information from the quantitative data analysis process is the responsibility of the student, and the formatting should adhere to the university formatting requirements.

Additional Guidelines for Outside Assistance. If you do decide to hire editors, statisticians, proofreaders, writing or dissertation coaches, and transcriptionists, keep in mind you should ask some important questions and clarify rules of communication and assistance boundaries.

1. Clarify expectations from the person you hire regarding cost, contracts, turnaround times, delivery methods, and finished work.

2. Discuss and adhere to the rules of communication. How you will obtain feedback? Most feedback will be included in your paper as tracked changes in Word, or a PDF file. You could also as for a bulleted list or matrix of suggested changes (what editor's call a Style Sheet). You should also discuss what methods of contact you should use to contact your editor should you have questions or concerns about the editing and revising process.

3. Provide the most up-to-date dissertation templates and guidelines for your university—especially to your editor.

4. Be sure each individual you hire is qualified to do the work necessary for your success. For example, editors should be an expert in the writing style (e.g., APA, MLA, or Chicago Style) and ask for a trial edit of three full pages of text. Statisticians should have a certificate or a degree in mathematics or a concentration in statistics. A transcriptionist is the most difficult person to obtain proof of experience. No matter whom you hire, ask for references, preferably someone you can speak to directly.

Remember that you have asked these individuals to assist you on your journey. Be open to the insights and perspectives of others, including your mentor and committee members! The people you have handpicked to work with you are the subject matter experts, and are experienced in the areas in need of review and revisions. Look at all the feedback you receive, from your team and university reviewers, as steps toward making your paper stronger and scholarly. Be positive!

A final warning when deciding to use outside services to assist you with your educational needs: There are many editing and dissertation coaching organizations listed on the Internet, and many are legitimate and ethical entities. However, be very aware that anyone who offers to edit, write, or complete your data analysis for you is overstepping the boundaries of ethical practices. Additionally, and most important, if you allow someone else to make permanent changes to the text and meaning of your thesis or dissertation, you run a very strong risk of a possible stern reprimand, completing a new project or research study, termination of your educational journey and exit from the university. The worst possibility is losing your degree and having a permanent note on your transcript of any or all of these consequences of unethical scholarship practices, and still having to pay any student loans for an education for which you will have no degree. With something this detrimental on your university transcripts, other universities may decline your request to attend classes, even for continuing education units needed for employment or promotions!

Be informed, be cautious, and **Keep it Simple, Scholars!**

CHAPTER 12

WHAT'S NEXT FOR YOU?

Congratulations, you are done! After you have completed your masters or doctoral journey and published your degree-bearing paper, what's next for you? Following are some great suggestions!

Publishing

Blogging. An exceptional way to continue writing, even if it is publishing one paragraph per week, blogging can keep you enjoined in your topic, and provide you with a followership of readers. The advent of social media created a minefield of opportunity to keep abreast of the development of your topic and create small statements or stories for other people interested in the same information following you. This form of networking is extremely beneficial and important for the next publication ideas in this section. Whatever you do, continue researching and writing to keep your mind sharp and your topic of interest at the fore!

Books. When your mentor told you to keep your thesis or dissertation simple, they may have told you to "wait to write your book until AFTER you are a master or doctor." If you think about this clearly, you should be able to discern why. If not, here is the reason for this saying: Not only will you have the ability to put "by Master or Doctor YOU" as the author of the book, you will also have the skills and experience to provide a sound novel on your topic. Additionally, you will be free from the encumbrances of the multitude of individuals involved in the thesis and dissertation writing process; that is, no IRB, no mentor and committee, no university Dean to go through for publication. Indeed, you will still work with editors, statisticians, transcriptionists, writing tutors, publishers but the process will be much easier, and you can write about your topic without being held back from meeting a publication or personal timeline goal. Also, be sure to obtain a copyright for all your work.

Journal Articles. After publishing your thesis or dissertation, begin adding to your professional publication portfolio by writing articles for scholarly journals. Collaborate with cohorts and former instructors to build on the various topics of interest something that will keep you moving forward as a scholar, practitioner, and life-long learner. Be sure to check the copyright and ownership of all of your work. It is highly recommended to obtain a copyright; however, some professional journals ask you to give them ownership of your article—that is a decision only you can make. Also, be wary of article publishers that might ask you for a fee. Double-check to be sure those organizations are legitimate; you could lose the copyright by submitting to some unethical organizations that will actually steal your intellectual property.

Presentations and Community Outreach

Mentoring. What better way to celebrate education and the attainment of a masters or doctoral degree than to work with up-and-coming students! Many people would welcome the encouragement and guidance from someone who once walked the same educational path. Whether you choose to start a tutoring service of your own, or just answer questions and be a social media cheerleader on educational online forums, giving back to other students provides a sense of goodwill and accomplishment that can be a shared experience with whomever you help.

Professional Organizations. Are you a great public speaker? If so, you have a great opportunity to go out into the world and educate other individuals interested in your topic! Many scholars find ways to obtain paid speaking engagements, and paired with publishing journal articles and books on your topic, you could increase your value in your related industry.

Teaching. One way for many scholars to give back to up-and-coming students is to become an adjunct or tenured professor at a community college or university, for both ground and online campuses. Some individuals are already teaching undergraduate courses when entering the doctoral program. However, the attainment of a doctoral degree provides the opportunity for people to teach at all levels of higher education, and thus, increase the number of courses they can teach.

Volunteerism. The obvious give back to one's community is to volunteer one's time and experience to help others. Perhaps among the other ideas listed here, you could offer one free online "how to" video, or help someone at no charge. Offering to assist with training at a non-profit organization could help with networking toward an invitation to give a presentation at another local organization. The possibilities are endless.

In summary, I hope this book has been helpful for you to keep it simple throughout your journey meet your scholarly and academic writing goals!

Finally, above all things…

Show humility and grace on your successful ascension in the world of scholars. Remember you were once at the bottom of the ladder; keep the vision of how much you struggled to get to the top. Help others achieve their goals and reap the rewards of knowing you helped someone else accomplish their dreams.

Go forth and do good things…

Be blessed by being the blessing. ~ Dr. Jules

REFERENCES

American Psychological Association (APA). (2009). *Publication Manual of the American Psychological Association* (6th ed.). American Psychological Association: Washington DC.

Bandura, A. (1986). Social foundations of thought and action. Englewood Cliffs, NJ: Prentice-Hall.

Barrett, K. (2016). Statistical Package for Social Sciences for Windows (SPSS). P. J. Lavrakas, (Ed). Encyclopedia of Survey Research Methods. Sage Publications. doi: 10.4135/9781412963947.n549

Brunson, L. (2014). Understanding successful small business decision-making during recessionary periods: A qualitative phenomenological study. Dissertation. University of Phoenix. ProQuest GradWorks. UMI 3692002

Collaborative Institutional Training Initiative (CITI) (2016).

   Collaborative Institutional Training Initiative at the University of

   Miami. Retrieved from https://www.citiprogram.org/

Cone, J., & Foster, S. (2006). *Dissertations and theses from start to finish*

   (2nd ed.). Washington, DC: American Psychological Association.

Creswell, J., W. (2009). Research design: Qualitative, quantitative, and

   mixed methods approaches (3rd ed.). Thousand Oaks, CA: Sage

   Publications Inc.

Department of Health and Human Services. (2016). Code of Federal

   Regulations; 45 CFR 46. Retrieved from

   http://www.hhs.gov/ohrp/humansubjects/guidance/45cfr46.ht

   ml

Esposito, J. L. (2010). Some Thoughts on the Use of Field Tests to

   Evaluate Survey Questionnaires. Bureau of Labor Statistics

   Retrieved from http://www.bls.gov/osmr/pdf/st100330.pdf

Fals-Borda. O. (1987). The Application of Participatory Action-

   Research in Latin America. *International Sociology, 2*(4), 329-347.

   http://dx.doi.org/10.1177/026858098700200401

Friese, S. (2012). *Qualitative data analysis with ATLAS.ti.* Thousand

   Oaks, California: Sage Publications Ltd.

Garner, B. A. (2009). *Garner's modern American usage*. Oxford
University Press: New York, N.Y.

Kane, T. S. (2000). *The Oxford essential guide to writing*. Berkley Books:
New York, NY.

Knowles, M., S., Holton, E. F., & Swanson, R. A. (1998). *The adult
learner: The definitive classic in adult education and human resource
development* (5th ed.). Houston: Gulf Professional Publishing.
doi: 10.1108/00197851211268045

Lester, M. & Beason, L. (2013). *The McGraw-Hill handbook of English
grammar and usage* (2nd ed.). McGraw-Hill: New York, NY.

Lincoln, Y. S. & Guba, E. G. (1985). Naturalistic Inquiry. Newbury
Park, CA: Sage Publications.

Maslow, A. (1943). A theory of human motivation. *Psychological Review,
50*, 370-396.

MAXQDA™ (2016). MASQDA Qualitative Data Analysis Software
for Windows and Mac OS X. Retrieved from
http://www.maxqda.com/products/new-in-maxqda-12

Merriam-Webster's Collegiate Dictionary (11th ed.). (2014). Merriam-
Webster, Incorporated, Springfield, MA.

Modern Language Association (MLA) Handbook for Writers of

    Research Papers (7th ed.). (2009)

Moustakas, C. (1994). *Phenomenological research methods.* Thousand Oaks,

    CA: Sage.

Perot, Y. M. (2013). Factors that determine the parental selection of a

    secondary school. Dissertation. Grand Canyon University.

    ProQuest GradWorks. UMI 3605260

QSR International. (2016). An overview of NVivo™. Retrieved from

    http://www.qsrinternational.com/product/NVivo11-for-

    Windows

The Chicago Manual of Style (CMS)(16th ed.). (2010). The University

    of Chicago Press: Chicago, IL.

Yin, R. K. (2009). *Case study research: Design and methods* (4th ed.).

    Thousand Oaks, CA: Sage Publications.

APPENDIXES

APPENDIX A: RESOURCE EXAMPLES

Other great sources for assistance not already included in the references include:

American Psychological Association style writing and formatting:

www.apa.org

https://owl.english.purdue.edu

http://isites.harvard.edu/icb/icb.do?keyword=apa_exposed

Doi numbers:

www.crossref.org

Grammar assistance: https://www.grammarly.com

Online surveys:

http://surveymonkey.com

https://www.surveygizmo.com/

Citation Records

Read Cube for citations:

https://www.readcube.com/home?r_c=dhnmn

Turnitin plagiarism reports

https://guides.turnitin.com/01_Manuals_and_Guides/Student/Student_User_Manual/17_Originality_Check

APPENDIX B: COMMITTEE MEMBER REQUEST EXAMPLE

Dear Dr._____:

Hello, my name is _____, and I am currently perusing a Doctoral degree in_____ with University of _____. I have just completed <u>(tell the person where you are in your journey)</u>. At this point in my doctoral journey, it has become necessary to find committee members who will help guide my path through the dissertation process. I believe your knowledge and expertise in _____will be very helpful as I study and conduct my research to support my topic.

My research topic is <u>"Fill this in with the title of your dissertation."</u> I am interested in this topic because_____. I intend to use a _____method and _____design.

Problem Statement:

Purpose Statement:

My goal is to complete my dissertation and use my research as a foundation for furthering the knowledge base and studies of <u>the subject of your topic.</u>

<u>Highlights of my Background</u>: CHANGE THIS SECTION TO FIT YOUR BACKGROUND

Master's Degree: Where and when?

I have worked in _____ for over _____years. I currently manage/teach/lead.

My Undergraduate degree is from _____where I majored in _____ and minored in_____.

My grade point average in my undergraduate classes was _____ and is currently _____.

I am currently enrolled in _____ were the primary focus is learning about team dynamics from a leadership perspective OR I am currently done with coursework and am ready for submission.

Because my dissertation is a long-time goal of mine, I am seeking committee members who will help me achieve this goal. I would appreciate your consideration to join my dissertation committee (along with my mentor, <u>Dr. ---only add this when looking for committee members and you already have a chair</u>). I believe my ability to listen and accept constructive criticism, straightforward attitude, and desire to succeed will be effective in your guiding me toward the completion of my dissertation.

Thank you for your time in advance.

Respectfully,

_____, Doctoral Student
University _____

APPENDIX C: PROSPECTUS OUTLINE EXAMPLE

Julie Ruff (Student at University of Phoenix)
(Dr. Julie Conzelmann)
Copyright December 19, 2009

1) **Dissertation topic**

   a) Title: Leadership recognition of organizational citizenship behaviors in the performance evaluation process.

   b) A review of current literature implies that no organizations are known to directly or explicitly recognize organizational citizenship behavior as part of the formal reward and recognition system. Therefore, the opportunity exists for organizational leaders to design and implement a performance evaluation process that officially recognizes the value of organizational citizenship behaviors exhibited by employees (Johnson, Holladay & Quinones, 2009).

2) **Significance**

   a) The significance of this study is to determine if employee productivity, teamwork, job satisfaction, and rewards are related to leadership formally recognizing employees who exhibit organizational citizenship behaviors as part of the performance evaluation process. The need to research, validate and improve systems to identify, reward, and retain the most qualified employees to meet the strategic needs of organizations is important to doctoral studies and organizational leadership theories as the world of business and direction of organizations change.

3) **Problem Statement**

   a) Organizational leaders rely on the human resources staff to recruit, train, retain, and reward employees with optimum knowledge, skills, and abilities (KSAs) but do not formally recognize the value added by employees who exhibit organizational citizenship behaviors, in addition to those expected as part of generic job descriptions and titles as provided at the time of hire.

4) **Purpose Statement**

   a) The purpose of this descriptive, quantitative study is to analyze the benefit of formally recognizing employees who exhibit organizational citizenship behaviors as part of the formal performance evaluation process. A random sample of 25 employees at each of 10 various organizations, to include employees holding management and non-management positions in healthcare, education, and retail organizations in Arizona, will determine whether or not leadership recognition of organizational citizenship behaviors positively affects employee productivity, teamwork, job satisfaction, and rewards.

5) **Research Questions**

   a) What are the benefits to the organization of formally recognizing employee's who exhibit organizational citizenship behaviors as part of the formal performance evaluation process for employees in education, healthcare, retail and government organizations in Arizona?

b) What are the consequences to the organization of formally recognizing employee's who exhibit organizational citizenship behaviors as part of the formal performance evaluation process for employees in education, healthcare, retail and government organizations in Arizona?

c) Will a perception of increased productivity, teamwork, job satisfaction, and organizational citizenship behavior exist by leaders due to the formal recognition of organizational citizenship behaviors for employees in education, healthcare, retail and government organizations in Arizona?

d) Will the implementation of formal recognition of organizational citizenship behaviors in performance evaluations cause employees to perceive an expectation of increased productivity, teamwork, job performance, rewards, and organizational citizenship behaviors in education, healthcare, retail, and government organizations in Arizona?

e) For this quantitative study the independent and dependent variables are:

   (1)   IV:

      (a)   Altruism: intrinsic desire to do the right thing

      (b)   Compliance: "good citizen" syndrome (Smith, Organ, & Near, 1983)

   (2)   DV:

      (a)   Productivity

      (b)   Teamwork

      (c)   Job satisfaction

      (d)   Cost

      (e)   Rate of turnover

6) **Research Method**
   a) The elements of the selected design will be descriptive and quantitative because the majority of available literature is relevant to obtaining information about employee productivity, teamwork, and job satisfaction. Employee productivity, teamwork, job satisfaction, cost, and rate of turnover can be measured and compared with information obtained from organizations regarding the recognition or lack of recognition of organizational citizenship behaviors. Therefore, a quantitative study may show whether or not organizations will benefit from leadership recognition and inclusion of organizational citizenship behaviors in formal job performance evaluations.

   b) Other variables may exist which can skew the outcome of the research study; therefore, a full list will be produced, the variables will be separated into two groups: independent variables (IV) and dependent variables (DV). All outlying data will be revealed but will not be part of the final data reported.

7) **Data Collection**
   a) ERIC Database website for peer-reviewed articles
   b) University of Phoenix library for peer-reviewed articles
   c) Peer-reviewed articles for supporting research documentation
   d) Peer-reviewed articles for primary research discovery

References

Bowen, D. E., & Inkpen, A. C. (2009). Exploring the role of "global mindset" in leading change in international contexts. *Journal of Applied Behavioral Science, 45.* 239. Retrieved from: Sage Publications database.

Chen, C., & Chiu, S. (2009, Fall). The mediating role of job involvement in the relationship between job characteristics and organizational citizenship behavior. *The Journal of Social Psychology, 149*(4), 474–494.

Chen, L., Niu, H., Wang, Y., Yang, C., & Tsaur, S. (2009). Does job standardization increase organizational citizenship behavior? *Public Personnel Management (38)*3. ABI/Inform Global.

Cooper, D. R., & Schindler, P. S. (2002). *Business research methods* (8th ed.). Boston: Irwin.

Creswell, J. W. (2002). *Educational research: Planning, conducting, and evaluating quantitative and qualitative research.* Upper Saddle River, NJ: Pearson.

Emerson, R. M. (1976). Social exchange theory. *Annual Review of Sociology,* (2)1, 335.

Ferris, G. R., Hochwarter, W. A., Buckley, M. R., Harrell-Cook, G.,

    & Frink, D. D. (1999). Human resources management: Some new

    directions. *Journal of Management, 25*(3), 385-415. Retrieved from

    Sage Publication database.

Griffin, J.D. (2012). Leadership Recognition of Organizational

    Citizenship Behaviors in Performance Evaluations in Washington

    State Healthcare Organizations. [Dissertation] University of

    Phoenix. Proquest: UMI 3534889.

Johnson, S. K., Holladay. E., & Quinones, M. A. (2009).

    Organizational citizenship behavior in performance evaluations:

    Distributive justice or injustice? *Journal of Business Psychology, (24)*,

    409-418. doi 10.1007/s10869-009-9118-0.

Kivlighan, D. (1997, March). Leader behavior and therapeutic gain:

    An application of situational leadership theory. *Group Dynamics:*

    Theory, Research, and Practice, 1(1), 32-38. Retrieved from

    EBSCOhost database.

Lengnick-Hall, C. A. & Lengnick-Hall, M. L. (1988). Strategic human

    resources management: A review of the literature and proposed

    typology. *Academy of Management: The Academy of Management Review,*

    13(3). 454. Retrieved from ProQuest database.

Leon, G. R., Kanfer, R., Hoffman, R.G., & Dupre, L. (1994). Group

    processes and task effectiveness in a Soviet-American expedition

    team. *Environment and Behavior, 26.* 149. Retrieved from Sage

    Publications database.

Li, C. & Hung, C. (2009). The influence of transformational

    leadership on workplace relationships and job performance. *Social*

    Behavior and Personality, 37(8), 1129-1142.

    doi 10.2224/sbp.2009.37.8.1129

Ruff, J. D. (2009). Prospectus. Student paper at University of

    Phoenix.

Russo, R. (2003). *Statistics for the behavioral sciences.* Taylor & Frances,

    Inc.

Schiffbauer, J., Barrett O'Brien, J., Timmons, B. K., & Kiarie, W. N.

    (2008). The role of leadership in HRH development in

    challenging public health settings. *Human Resources for Health.*

    Retrieved from Academic OneFile. Gale. Apollo Library,

    http://find.galegroup.com/ips/start.do?prodId=IPS

Smith, C. A., Organ, D. W., & Near, J. P. (1983). Organizational

    citizenship behavior: Its nature and antecedents. *Journal of Applied*

    Psychology, 68, 653–663.

Sun, L., Aryee, S., & Law, K. S. (2007, Jun). High-performance

human resource practices, citizenship behavior, and

organizational performance: a relational perspective. *Academy of*

*Management Journal, (50)*3, 558-577. (*AN 25525821*).

Toh, S. M., Morgeson, F. P., & Campion, M. A. (2008). Human

resources configurations: Investigating fit with the organizational

context. *Journal of Applied Psychology, 93*(4). 864-882. Retrieved

from ProQuest database.

**Note: This prospectus outline example is the beginning dissertation document created by Julie Ruff, a doctoral student at University of Phoenix in 2009. The information contained herein was submitted as an assignment as a student, is part of the published dissertation and book, *Leadership Recognition of Organizational Citizenship Behaviors in Performance Evaluations in Washington State Healthcare Organizations*, copyright 2012 and 2015, by Dr. Julie (Griffin) Conzelmann, all rights reserved.

APPENDIX D: RESEARCH PLAN EXAMPLE

Individual Research Study Plan
Julie Ruff (Student at University of Phoenix)
(Dr. Julie Conzelmann)
Copyright January 2010

Problem Statement

The subject of leadership understanding the human resources tools available to run a successful organization varies from the human resources aspect of this understanding. Organizational leaders rely on the human resources staff to recruit, train, and retain employees with optimum knowledge, skills, and abilities (KSAs) but are lacking in recognizing if this is successfully accomplished.

Over the past 4 years, culminating in the recent events in the economy, the demise of job opportunities across the country have increased. This implies that organizations will be narrowing down employment opportunities that fit specifically to those KSAs necessary for organizations to function. Employing the least amount of full-time employees (FTEs) equipped with a portfolio of KSAs,

91

organizations will lower operating, administrative and payroll costs, while increasing or stabilizing the productivity of the organization.

Organizations recruit or promote employees to perform activities necessary for the successful operation of the organization. However, the basis for employing one person over another in a position is the qualifications one holds versus those necessary to perform the duties of the position. Important are the KSAs, to include personal experiences, training, and education

Generally, prospective employees receive a description of tasks and duties. The sometimes lengthy and arduous task of determining the best candidates to hire may lead to a disparity of the requisite KSAs versus those the candidate is able to use to the extent needed by the organization. In this light, organizations can better identify discrepancies in what needs to be done, such as what skill sets are necessary to perform specific jobs in specific areas or industries.

One line of research will be to identify positions with highly complicated and specific skills that are required in order for the organization to be successful and compare this with the skills of the employee who holds these positions. Assuming the organization already uses some form of human resources software, updating the organizational database can help match employee KSAs with job descriptions (Schiffbauer, Barrett O'Brien, Timmons, & Kiarie, 2008). Additionally, identifying employees holding the required KSAs but underutilized in the organization can assist with having the right employee performing not only to his or her potential but also to the increased benefit of the organization.

The Importance to Doctoral Study

The need to research, validate, and improve systems to identify the best qualified employees for specific organizations is important to doctoral studies as the world of business and direction of organizations change. As these global changes arise, the most up-to-date, valid and reliable research will provide data and solutions on current issues facing organizations, identify opportunities for improving organizational human resources, identify future leadership needs, and set the stage for future research on this subject. For example, a study conducted by Schiffbauer, Barrett O'Brien, Timmons, and Kiarie (2008), research existed with regard to leadership managing and understanding human resources issues in various countries. However, the majority of research available centers on health related issues, limiting the usefulness of the research and

93

design in other industries. The analysis and design of a doctoral study in this regard should have the flexibility of design to be useful in any organizational setting.

A sound doctoral study will research the need for and changes in Enterprise Resource Planning, workforce analysis specifically in critical roles: healthcare, engineering, geology, banking, and education, environmental analysis, strategic planning, goal setting, benchmarking, and best practices. The ideal outcome will be to determine if these tools are beneficial to organizations and if so, to design and implement a study which provides an outcome specifying a valid, reliable, and optimum solution for the betterment of the organizational use of human resources, to be included as published, expert subject matter in future foundational doctoral research.

The Importance to Business Management Leadership

This subject is important to business management leadership, as organizations will be downsizing FTEs and will rely on quality research and subject matter expert advice with regard to organizational staffing necessary for successful operation of organizations. If one approached an organization offering to assist with a study of how the organization determines the performance needs of a division or specific job, and how the organization equates the qualifications of prospective employees, one should provide valid and reliable research on the subject. Additionally, in providing one's own valid research methodologies as a subject matter expert, organizational leaders may be open to assistance more so than if one were not able to prove qualitative and quantitative information based on sound research.

Providing solutions for expected organizational issues is necessary and requires constant research for optimum success of organizations. Since leaders must decide whether to outsource jobs or not and if so, using societal and demographical information to identify the best location to do so is expected. Organizations must be ready to match the right people with the right skills to complete necessary tasks and provide continuity of training and educational opportunities for personal and organizational success. Additionally, succession planning is extremely important to the overall success of organizations (Schiffbauer, Barrett O'Brien, Timmons, & Kiarie, 2008). In identifying the best skilled employees, grooming them over time within the organization and toward organizational goals, the recognition of future leaders within the organization could help with creating the continuity of business performance and lowering the stress of change among organizational management.

Many organizations depend on hiring employees to perform necessary tasks that enable the organizations to reach strategic goals. Hiring employees with the knowledge, skills, abilities, experience, and education is necessary to produce and sell goods and services at a profit to the organization. A disparity may exist in the selection and placement of employees with regard to the KSAs and the description and duties of the position for which employees are hired.

When employees attain positions where the KSAs outweigh the required tasks, or the tasks outweigh the KSAs, organizations experience a loss of production and revenue. This affects organizations, employees, vendors, and consumers. Department leaders and managers may be interested in a study of the impact on organizations in regard to how well matched employee KSAs are to the required job description and tasks performed.

Purpose Statement

The purpose of this descriptive, quantitative study is to analyze the relationship between the KSAs of employees to job descriptions and tasks for a random sample of 25 employees at each of 10 various organizations. The representative organizations will include healthcare, education, and retail organizations in Arizona. The expected method of obtaining data is through an anonymous survey requesting a personal assessment of individual participant KSAs, experience, and education and providing participants the opportunity to rate current job satisfaction. Additionally, a detailed job description and a list of required KSAs for each position surveyed are necessary from each organization's human resources department.

The selection of participants and organizations will commence by first asking for permission and recruiting volunteers through the organization's human resources department, to include providing the requisite permission and assurance of confidentiality. The information obtained will be collected and sorted by KSAs, education, experience, and job satisfaction ratings. One possible outcome of this study is to determine whether employees' KSAs match and relate to job descriptions and tasks; this will make it possible to determine if KSAs link to organizational leadership strategies, to compare current human resource and leadership trends, and identify possible solutions.

Research Question and Hypotheses

This quantitative study will answer one research question and test one alternative hypothesis to determine the relationship between the identification, matching, and use of KSAs with employee productivity and job satisfaction. The objective is to ensure the research considers the various areas of influence while staying within the specific direction proposed in the problems statement (Cooper, 2002).

Research Question: How does matching KSAs to job descriptions and tasks relate to productivity and job satisfaction for employees in education, healthcare, retail and government organizations in Arizona?

This is the main question that must be answered in order to understand the current state of employee matching to productivity and job satisfaction and determine if a need exists for improvements and identify possible solutions. The significance of this study is to determine if employee productivity and job satisfaction relate to matching employee KSAs to job descriptions and tasks. Therefore, the objective of the research study will be to prove or disprove the following hypotheses:

H⁰: There is no significant difference in productivity and satisfaction when KSAs relate to job descriptions and tasks for employees in educational, healthcare, retail and government organizations in Arizona.

H¹: Employees in educational, healthcare, retail and government organizations in Arizona whose KSAs relate to job descriptions and tasks will have increased productivity and job satisfaction than an employee whose KSAs are not matched to job descriptions and tasks. A dilemma may exist with regard to testing the hypotheses. Russo (2003) suggested the null hypothesis, $H^{0,}$ should be tested using a two-tailed approach where a determination to accept or reject the null hypothesis is based on the standard normal distribution z score between, -1.96 and 1.96. However, Russo (2003) also indicates that with the possibility of testing more than one hypothesis, lopsided testing may increase the validity of the result to either accept or reject the null hypothesis, and the alternative hypothesis studied, to answer the research question accurately.

Literature Review

Bowen and Inkpen's (2009) qualitative and exploratory study investigated the influence of effective leadership in change processes in cross-cultural organizations from a global perspective (Bowen & Inkpen, 2009). Emerging research over the past 10 years indicate the characteristics of intellectual, social and psychological intelligence lead to effective leadership behaviors and a global mindset. The findings of the descriptive data collected through individual surveys of executives, college professor and alumni indicates a link between a global mindset and individual performance. Due to economic changes the organization of study, specifically the Johnson and Johnson Company, used the leadership change to a global mindset to implement employee empowerment, succession and job placement planning, and improved production processes. After implementation, organizational culture, employee perceptions, and adaptability to changes showed a slow but significant improvement.

Ferris, Hochwarter, Buckley, Harrell-Cook, and Frink (1999) provided a qualitative study that reviews the early concepts of human resources management (HRM) over approximately 80 years. The progress of HRM from overseeing hiring practices to the strategic practices of organizations, which align employees, jobs, and tasks with the strategies of organizations, happened only in the past 10-15 years. Current HRM trends change constantly due to global, technological, and political influences. The HRM theories have changed constantly but not consistently, leaving too many assumptions regarding best practices. Is a pattern or universalistic HRM perspective a possible better fit for organizations? Consistency, flexibility, and effectiveness are factors of constraints on improving HRM, and these factors must not negatively affect competitive priorities. With staffing being the most important challenge for organizations, individuals should be the most important unit of analysis, followed by leadership influence and politics.

Leaders must be flexible when changing from tasking relationships to relationship building within groups. Kivlighan (1997) conducted this quantitative study hypothesizing there is a correlation between leadership dimensions with group atmosphere, suggesting that leaders should attempt to establish group norms in the early stages. Changing norms as group member's progress toward resolution or completion of tasks is difficult to change. The study used a Likert Scale questionnaire to gather data; however, the study has a mono-method bias because the study was conducted using the researcher's organization and information was obtained from an internal perspective. The results of this study indicate the hypothesis is correct: leaders need to use a flexible leadership style. If the study were repeated, the outcome may or may not be different if the research study had included information from a variety of external organizations.

A review of this mixed study provides an objective to measure group functioning and effectiveness in a highly task-oriented setting. Through individual and group interviews Leon, Kanfer, Hoffman, and Dupre (1994) assessed the effects of the environment, climate, extended proximity to group members, personalities, gender, ethnicity, nationality, and physical dynamics (health and stress), on group effectiveness. Perceptions of the group relative to specific tasks were generally negative, although most members stated that communication was the most positive of the relationships among the group members.

The results of the interviews indicate a disparity within the group regarding gender ethnicity and nationality on group effectiveness during encounters with members of villages along the expedition route. Perceptions of "cliques," where the men, women, Caucasian or Russian participants excluded the remaining group members for tasks or decision-making, created adverse situations among the group. Leon et al., (1994) used an extreme situation to research group cohesiveness, effectiveness, and functioning; however, replication of the study could occur under normal work-related conditions to determine the overall effectiveness and functioning of tasks for groups within organizations and be useful to further research.

Lengnick-Hall and Lengnick-Hall (1988) conducted a qualitative study that investigated if HRM is separate from a functional level than an organizational leadership level and differentiating content issues from process elements where HRM is concerned. The historical review of available literature, including Dyer (1985), examined past human resources approaches reporting the expectation of remaining constant over time, and only organizational strategies change (Lengnick-Hall & Lengnick-Hall, 1988). Therefore, when organizational strategy changes will the human resources strategy change; human resources strategy does not affect organizational strategies.

Organizational leaders must assume all human resources choices are variable based on economic conditions, costs, strategies, and business choices. Of the three hypotheses provided by Lengnick-

Hall and Lengnick-Hall (1988), the topic of number three may be beneficial for further study:

Hypothesis 3: Firms that engage in a strategy formulation process that systematically and reciprocally considers human resources and competitive strategy will perform better (using multiple measures of effectiveness) over the long term than firms that manage human resources primarily as a means to solve competitive strategy issues. (p. 468)

Toh, Morgeson, and Campion, (2008) identified five hypotheses related to the use of human resources practices in conjunction with other complimentary practices or "bundling" (p. 864) in this quantitative study. Current literature findings determined that bundles are a better process for human resources to use because they can be researched better and provide consistent data in comparison to practices based on individual human resources practices. The current study suggests using bundles for key human resources practices: staffing, development, rewards and evaluation (Toh, Morgeson, & Campion, 2008). Interviews and questionnaires were the data collection method in this large-scale study (661 organizations with upwards of 6,000 employees). A cluster analysis helped to determine the variables between costs, motivation, and deciding which practices were most appropriate for bundling. Moreover, a secondary expected result of the research is to determine if organization logic regarding culture and organizational strategy will become consistent based on bundling human resources processes (Toh, Morgeson, & Campion, 2008).

Theoretical Framework

From the basic literature review, the theoretical framework consists of arguing that employee KSAs need to relate to job descriptions and tasks. Moreover, an argument exists that matching KSAs to job descriptions and tasks have a significant relationship to increased productivity and job satisfaction. The past data provided by Ferris et al. (1999) suggested that hiring practices that align employee skills with organizational needs is a relatively new concept. With the ever changing policies and technologies hiring and retention practices may not have moved forward exponentially with the needs of organizations. Leadership decisions may have an effect on hiring practices; however, the current literature does not provide enough information to determine if this has an effect on organizational hiring practices (Ferris et al., 1999)

Lengnick-Hall and Lengnick-Hall (1988) confirmed that human resources approaches had become stagnant and no strategies had been studied to improve human resources policies because an assumption existed that when the organizational strategy changed so should the human resources strategy. Additionally, Kanfer, Hoffman, and Dupre (1994) interject important variables for consideration in human resources strategies: the effects of the environment, climate, extended proximity to group members, personalities, gender, ethnicity, nationality, and physical dynamics (health and stress), on group effectiveness. Furthermore, Toh, Morgeson, and Campion (2008) identified several additional variables that are important to human resources strategies: staffing, development, rewards, and evaluation.

Method and Design

The elements of the selected design will be descriptive and quantitative given that the majority of available literature thus far is relevant to matching employee KSAs to job descriptions and tasks. Many variables exist which can skew the outcome of the research study; therefore, a full list will be produced and the variables will be separated into three groups: independent variables, dependent variables, and control variables. Those variables that have little or no impact on the outcome of the study will be listed as outlying information but will be included in the statistical data to show all relevant variables were researched and tested. This will provide validity and reliability to the tests. The minimum suggested statistical methodologies are multiple-regression analysis, ANOVA, and a descriptive analysis, and a covariance analysis to determine if any independent or dependent variables affect any identified control variables. Tables and charts will be available for reviewing the data analysis methods and outcomes.

Selection of the participants will be from 10 random organizations in Arizona, representing healthcare, education, and retail organizations. Each organization will have at least 100 employees who agree to participate in the study. Of those organizations, 25 random employees will be asked to participate in at least two anonymous surveys. An assurance of confidentiality and statement that participation is optional will be provided to all participants. The information collected through the surveys will be sorted and analyzed using the various forms of statistical analysis to determine if any independent or dependent variables exist. The results from both analyses will be disseminated and the outcome revealed regarding proving the null hypothesis or accepting the alternative hypothesis.

References

Bowen, D. E., & Inkpen, A. C. (2009). Exploring the role of "global mindset" in leading change in international contexts. *Journal of Applied Behavioral Science, 45*. 239. Retrieved from: Sage Publications database.

Cooper, D. R., & Schindler, P. S. (2002). *Business research methods* (8th ed.). Boston: Irwin.

Creswell, J. W. (2002). *Educational research: Planning, conducting, and evaluating quantitative and qualitative research*. Upper Saddle River, NJ: Pearson.

Ferris, G. R., Hochwarter, W. A., Buckley, M. R., Harrell-Cook, G., & Frink, D. D. (1999). Human resources management: Some new directions. *Journal of Management, 25*(3), 385-415. Retrieved from Sage Publication database.

Griffin, J. D. (2012). Leadership Recognition of Organizational Citizenship Behaviors in Performance Evaluations in Washington State Healthcare Organizations. [Dissertation] University of Phoenix. Proquest: UMI 3534889.

Kivlighan, D. (1997, March). Leader behavior and therapeutic gain:

    An application of situational leadership theory. *Group Dynamics:*

    Theory, Research, and Practice, 1(1), 32-38. Retrieved from

    EBSCOhost database.

Leon, G. R., Kanfer, R., Hoffman, R.G. & Dupre, L. (1994). Group

    processes and task effectiveness in a Soviet-American expedition

    team. *Environment and Behavior, 26.* 149. Retrieved from Sage

    Publications database.

Lengnick-Hall, C. A., & Lengnick-Hall, M. L. (1988). Strategic human

    resources management: A review of the literature and proposed

    typology. *Academy of Management: The Academy of Management*

    Review, 13(3). 454. Retrieved from ProQuest database.

Ruff, J. D. (2009). Prospectus. Student paper at University of

    Phoenix.

Ruff, J. D. (2009). Individual research study plan. Student paper at

    University of Phoenix.

Russo, R. (2003). *Statistics for the behavioral sciences.* Taylor & Frances,

    Inc.

Schiffbauer, J., Barrett O'Brien, J., Timmons, B. K., & Kiarie, W. N.

(2008). The role of leadership in HRH development in

challenging public health settings. *Human Resources for Health.*

Retrieved from Academic OneFile. Gale. Apollo Library.

Retrieved from

http://find.galegroup.com/ips/start.do?prodId=IPS

Toh, S. M., Morgeson, F. P., & Campion, M. A. (2008). Human

resources configurations: Investigating fit with the organizational

context. *Journal of Applied Psychology, 93*(4). 864-882. Retrieved

from ProQuest database.

**Note: This prospectus outline example is the beginning dissertation document created by Julie Ruff, a doctoral student at University of Phoenix in 2009. The information contained herein was submitted as an assignment as a student, and is part of the published dissertation and book, *Leadership Recognition of Organizational Citizenship Behaviors in Performance Evaluations in Washington State Healthcare Organizations*, copyright 2012 and 2015, by Dr. Julie (Griffin) Conzelmann, all rights reserved.

APPENDIX E: DISSERTATION FORMAT EXAMPLE

Following is an APA formatted example of a dissertation. Remember that your university may have other formatting requirements. Use the template provided by your university, or use this format and the APA manual as a guide.

A dissertation usually has four basic elements: front matter, chapters, references, and back matter. Each elemental section has various page and formatting requirements. The elements and their contents are listed below.

Front matter: Title page, signature page, abstract, acknowledgments, dedication, table of contents, list of tables, list of figures, other lists, and preface. The title page, signature page, and preface require a section break after the last letter of text. All other pages use a page break.

Chapters: This section contains the five main chapters of the research project. Each chapter is separated by a page break.

References: This section contains a list of all the references used in the research. The references are listed in alphabetical order by first author name. The formatting for each reference is dictated by the formatting style used by each university. For APA, the examples for references are on pages 192 through 224. This section is followed by a page break.

Back matter: The last section of the dissertation includes the appendixes and may include a list of footnotes and an author biography. The appendixes are usually the permissions and other supporting documents for the dissertation process. The footnotes may refer to specific information in the text of the chapters. The author biography may or may not be required by your university.

Again, be sure to check with your university and use any templates and manuals provided and required to format your paper. Be sure to provide your hired assistants, especially your editor, with the most recent approved dissertation guide and formatting document. These documents are helpful for double-checking your paper meets your university's required elements, and is the final step in preparing your paper for approval submissions and final publication.

TITLE PAGE

NAME OF YOUR DISSERTATION HERE

by

Your Name Here

Copyright Year

Name of Your University

**Note: Use the template for your university for your title page

SIGNATURE PAGE

NAME OF YOUR DISSERTATION HERE

Approved for Publication

Month and Year

APPROVED BY:

First Last, PhD, Chairperson

First Last, PhD, Committee Member

First Last, PhD, Committee Member

_____

First Last

_____

First Last

_____

First Last

_____

Important Person, PhD
Title, Area of Importance
Name of University

*Note: Use the signature page as designed by your specific university

ABSTRACT

Starts flush left, double-spaced, 250 words or less (or up to 350, depending on your university requirements). Must include all elements from Chapters 1 – 5.

1. Chapter 1: This is the problem; this is the purpose of the study.

2. Chapter 2: This is what the literature said about the topic.

3. Chapter 3: This is the method and design chosen; this was the population sample, this was the geographic location.

4. Chapter 4: This is what the findings were.

5. Chapter 5: This is what one can conclude from conducting the research. This is the area where future research should focus on this topic.

DEDICATION

This element is not included until obtaining Dean's approval

Family

Friends

Co-learners

ACKNOWLEDGMENTS

This element is not included until obtaining Dean's approval

Chair

Committee Member

Committee Member

Others who inspired you

Others who assisted you (statistician, editor, coach, transcriptionist)

TABLE OF CONTENTS

Contents	Page

List of Tables	x
List of Figures	x
Other Lists	x
Preface	x
Chapter 1: Introduction	x
Background of the Problem	x
Statement of the Problem	x
Purpose of the Study	x
Significance of the Problem	x
Significance of the study	x
Significance of the study to leadership	x
Nature of the Study	x
Overview of the research method	x
Overview of the design appropriateness	x
Description of Research Focus	x
Research Question	x
Hypothesis	x
Theoretical Framework	x
Definition of Terms	x
Assumptions	x
Scope	x
Limitations	x

Delimitations...x

Conclusion...x

Summary..x

Chapter 2: Review of the Literature...x

    Title Searches, Books, Articles, Research Documents, and Journals....................x

    History of Topic..x

    Theories...x

    Gap in the Literature...x

    Conclusion..x

    Summary...x

Chapter 3: Methodology...x

    Research Method and Design Appropriateness.......................................x

        Elaboration and rational for research method..................................x

        Elaboration and rational for research design...................................x

    Research Questions..x

    Hypothesis (quantitative)...x

    Sample Population...x

    Geographic Location..x

    Sampling...x

    Informed Consent..x

    Confidentiality..x

    Instrumentation...x

        Appropriateness for instrumentation for this study...........................x

120

Permissions needed to use instrumentation x

Pilot study x

Data Collection x

Validity and Reliability x

Internal validity x

External validity x

Reliability x

Data Analysis x

Conclusion x

Summary x

Chapter 4: Results x

Findings x

Conclusion x

Summary x

Chapter 5: Conclusions and Recommendations x

Review of the Problem x

Summary of the Literature x

Conducting the Research x

Review of the Findings x

Conclusions from the Findings x

Implications x

Recommendations for Future Research x

Conclusion x

121

Summary x

References x

Footnotes x

Appendix A: Permissions x

Appendix B: Letter of Recruitment x

Appendix C: Informed Consent Form x

Appendix D: Permission to Use an Existing Survey x

Appendix D: Permission to Use Archived Data x

Appendix E: Original Survey Instrument x

Appendix F: Modified Survey Instrument (if permission to modify is granted) x

Author Biography x

**Note: These elements are not all necessary nor used for all universities. Always double-check the elements and appendixes required by your specific university and the levels of headings required for the table of contents.

LIST OF TABLES

Table 1: x

Table 2: x

LIST OF FIGURES

Figure 1 x

Figure 2 x

124

OTHER LISTS

This is optional

PREFACE

This is optional

Chapter 1

Introduction

Background of the Problem

Statement of the Problem

Purpose of the Study

Significance of the Problem

Significance of the study.

Significance of the study to leadership.

Nature of the Study

Overview of the research method.

Overview of the design appropriateness.

Description of Research Focus

Research Question

RQ1:

Sub-question (qualitative)

SQ1:

Hypothesis(es) (quantitative)

$H1_a$:

$H1_0$:

Theoretical or Conceptual Framework

Definition of Terms: MUST include citations for all definitions, no exceptions!

Assumptions

Scope

Limitations

Delimitations

Conclusion

1. Discussion reflects a conclusion derived from the analysis of the topic.

2. Provide supporting citations for key points.

3. Present information in a discussion context, rather than simply stating or listing the information.

Summary:

1. Discussion summarizes key points presented in Chapter 1.

2. Provide supporting citations for key points.

3. Chapter summary ends with transition discussion/sentence to next chapter.

4. Present information in a discussion context, rather than simply stating or listing the information.

Chapter 2
(Chapter Level Header-Centered at Top of the Page See-APA Manual p. 62; however, follow your university requirements for levels of headings, which may vary from this format)

Literature Review (Level 1 Header)

Title Searches, Books, Articles, Research Documents, and Journals

History of Topic (Level 2 Header, flush left)

Fill in as much information about your topic from before the Big Bang until yesterday. Outlining and including your citations can help you know what you need to write about and where. The levels of headings can be found in the APA manual page 62.

Historical introduction of theory one. Start text here (Level 3 Header)

Theory definitions. Start text here (Level 4 Header)

a. Smith et al (1983) Organizational Citizenship Behavior

b. Feldman (1996) Management Theory

c. Giblin & Amuso (1997) Corporate Value Systems

More theories. Start text here (Level 5 Header)

a. Social Exchange Theory

b. Baeza (2009) Charismatic leadership

Theories: Supported by the Theoretical or Conceptual Framework in Chapter 1

Theories: Contrasting to literature supporting your topic in Chapter

Gap in the Literature

Conclusion

1. Discussion reflects a conclusion derived from the analysis of the literature review.

2. Provide supporting citations for key points.

3. Present information in a discussion context, rather than simply stating or listing the information.

Summary

1. Discussion summarizes key points presented in Chapter 2.

2. Provide supporting citations for key points.

3. Chapter summary ends with transition discussion/sentence to next chapter.

4. Present information in a discussion context, rather than simply stating or listing the information.

Chapter 3

Method

Research Method and Design Appropriateness

Elaboration and Rationale for Research Method.

Elaboration and Rationale for Research Design.

Research Question

RQ1:

Sub-question (qualitative)

SQ1:

Hypothesis(es) (quantitative)

$H1_a$:

$H1_0$:

Sample Population

Geographic Location

133

Sampling

Informed Consent

Confidentiality

Instrumentation

Appropriateness for Instrumentation for this Study.

Permissions needed to use instrumentation: If using an existing validated survey

Pilot study: Necessary if you create your own survey instrument; not necessary if using an existing validated survey

Data Collection

Validity and Reliability

Internal Validity (quantitative)

External Validity (quantitative)

Reliability (quantitative)

Credibility (qualitative)

Transferability (qualitative)

Dependability (qualitative)

Confirmability (qualitative)

Data Analysis Process

Conclusion

1. Discussion reflects a conclusion derived from the analysis of the method and design of the study.

2. Provide supporting citations for key points.

3. Present information in a discussion context, rather than simply stating or listing the information.

Summary:

1. Discussion summarizes key points presented in Chapter 3.

2. Provide supporting citations for key points.

3. Chapter summary ends with transition discussion/sentence to next chapter.

4. Present information in a discussion context, rather than simply stating or listing the information.

Chapter 4

Results

Findings

Conclusion

1. Discussion reflects a conclusion derived from the analysis of the data.

2. Provide supporting citations for key points.

3. Present information in a discussion context, rather than simply stating or listing the information.

Summary:

1. Discussion summarizes key points presented in Chapter 4.

2. Provide supporting citations for key points.

3. Chapter summary ends with transition discussion/sentence to next chapter.

4. Present information in a discussion context, rather than simply stating or listing the information.

Chapter 5

Conclusions and Recommendations

Review of the Problem

Summary of the Literature

Conducting the research

Review of the Findings

Conclusions

Implications

Recommendations for Future Research

Conclusion

1. Discussion reflects a conclusion derived from the analysis of the entire paper, from Chapters 1 – 4.

2. Provide supporting citations for key points.

3. Present information in a discussion context, rather than simply stating or listing the information.

Summary:

1. Discussion summarizes key points presented in Chapter 5.

2. Provide supporting citations for key points.

3. Chapter summary ends with transition discussion/sentence to next chapter.

4. Present information in a discussion context, rather than simply stating or listing the information.

REFERENCES

Footnotes

Optional

AUTHOR BIOGRAPHY

Optional: Only to be added at the time of Dean's review

submission if your university allows this page.

**Note: This template does not represent the format for any particular university but is only representative of the APA manual 6th edition formatting. Check with your specific university for the most recent required formatting policy and manual.

APPENDIX F: LIST OF POSSIBLE REQUIRED DOCUMENTS

Some food for thought, scholars: many students forget to append required documents to the proposal or final thesis or dissertation. Double-check with your university and mentor about which documents you might need to provide with your paper. Remember to be sure all documents have the required signatures and most recent date. Some university have specific policies about how recent dates must be on certain documents. Following are only some usual and customary documents for theses and dissertations; however, you should ensure you have the correct and completed documents!

- Letter of Authenticity or Originality
- Confidentiality Agreement
- Informed Consent for 18 Years and Over
- Letter of Parental Consent for 17 Years and Younger
- Permission to Use Archived Data
- Permission to Use Premises
- Letter of Recruitment
- Non-disclosure Agreement
- Letter of Collaboration for Academic Institutions
- Institutional Review Board (IRB) Application
- Permission to use an Existing Survey
- Request for Non-University Committee Member
- Oral Defense Documents

APPENDIX G: PARTICIPANT WITHDRAWAL EXAMPLE

By signing this withdrawal form, I hereby remove myself from the study entitled:_____. I understand that my identity will be protected, information collected because of my participation will be kept confidential, and that all documentation and electronic information will be destroyed.

My signature below acknowledges my intentions to withdraw from the study.

Signature of participant:_____

Date:_____

Study Participation Number:_____

Reason for withdrawal (voluntary, not required):_____

_____

E-mail this document to _____at _____@email.edu

APPENDIX H: FIELD TEST FEEDBACK EXAMPLE

Field Test Results

Field Test Qualifications

Field Test Respondent

Name_____

Credentials, Experience, and Relevant Training_____

Suggestions and Comments

Your SME should review and offer comments and revisions as necessary:

1. Questions should produce rich detail pertaining to the topic.
2. Weave definitions into the script.
3. In addition to the strengths, include any negativity associated with the experience.
4. Look at the strengths and challenges of the topic.
5. Readability and comprehension level of questions for participants.

6. Grade level of questions should be appropriate for sample population.
7. Focus on the language used in questions.
8. Questions should be conversational rather than scripted interrogations.
9. As the researcher, put the interviewees at ease.
10. Reassure participant responses are important to your research.

I have reviewed the interview questions for the research study titled:

_____

and have provided the suggested changes as noted above.

Signed_____Dated_____

APPENDIX I: LETTER OF RECRUITMENT EXAMPLE

Dear Esteemed Colleague,

I am a doctoral candidate at _____, working toward a Doctor of _____ Degree. I am conducting a research study entitled: _____ The purpose of the research study is to_____.

Your participation involves the completion of an interview/survey containing ## questions. Your participation in this study is voluntary, and should take no more than XX minutes to complete. If you choose not to participate or withdraw from the study at any time, you can do so without penalty. The results will be maintained in confidence.

As a participant in this study you may decline to participate or withdraw at any time without consequences. Confidentiality of your identity is guaranteed at all times. Data collected will be analyzed, presented, and reported in the dissertation with assurance that anonymity of your name and any other identifying characteristics are protected. Data will be stored in a secure locked area and will be held for a period XX years, and then be destroyed.

Although you may not personally profit, the possible benefit of your participation is a contribution to_____
_____.

Your Name

Doctoral Candidate, University _____

**Note: If you use a flyer you create, be sure to get permission to use other individuals' photos or likeness, copyright permissions from owners, or use open access photos.

ABOUT THE AUTHOR

Dr. Conzelmann embraces teaching, editing, and mentoring because these activities stimulate intellectual camaraderie, argumentation, and cooperative problem solving and lay the groundwork for life-long collaborative practice. She demonstrates curiosity and passion about a subject area to motivate students to learn. Collaborating with enthusiastic faculty rooted in servant and transformational leadership enhances scholarship, teaching, and learning through diversity and teamwork. Teaching, editing, and mentoring bring Dr. Conzelmann great joy, fulfilling a desire to leave the world in a better state:

"To leave the world a bit better, whether by a healthy child, a garden patch, or a redeemed social condition; to know that even one life has breathed easier because you have lived - that is to have succeeded"
~ Ralph Waldo Emerson

With an extensive 30-year background in leadership, mentoring, writing, and editing to include grant writing; creating, editing, and revising legislative statutes; correspondence and communications for a Department of Defense contractor; and 12 years of academic writing, Dr. Julie Conzelmann is also an accomplished and effective teacher, public speaker, and author. Dr. Conzelmann earned her doctorate in Management, specializing in Organizational Leadership, from the University of Phoenix in 2012, and Copyeditor's Certification from the University of California San Diego in 2015, she provides editorial guidance to both academic and private authors. In her spare time, Dr. Conzelmann enjoys writing, going for walks with her husband on the trails and beaches near their home on Camano Island, Washington.

Note: Author of *Leadership Recognition of Organizational Citizenship Behaviors in Performance Evaluations in Washington State Healthcare Organizations*: Available on Amazon.com

Index

Abbreviations 42
About the Author 150
Acknowledgments i
Acronyms 42
Additional Guidelines for Outside Assistance 68
Affect 42
Alternative Hypothesis (H1ᵃ) .... *See* Hypothesis
American Psychological Association 80
American Psychological Association (APA) Manual 1
Anthropomorphism 43
Appendixes 44
Appropriateness for Instrumentation for this Study 29
Atlas.ti™ 33
Background of the Problem 17
Backup 3
Blogging 71
Books 71
Bracketing 33
Case Study 24
Chapter 1 .... 1, 4
Chapter 2 4
Chapter 3 .... 4, 7
Chapter 4 .... 5, 11
Chapter 5 .... 5, 14
Chapter 6 17
Chapter 7 23
Chapter 8 36
Chapter 9 40
Chapter 10 60
Chapter 11 64
Chapter 12 71
Chicago Manual of Style (CMS) 1
Citation Records 80
Citations. 61
Collaborative Institutional Training Initiative 27
Committee 7, 9
Committee Member Request Example 81
Committee Request LetteR 10
Community Outreach 73
Concepts 15
Conceptual Framework 20
Conclusion 15, 22, 35, 39, 129, 131, 135, 137, 139
Conclusion, Implications, & Recommendations for Further Research 37
Conclusions from the Findings 38

Conducting the Research 38
Confidentiality 27
Confidentiality Agreement 144
Confirmability 32
Credibility 32
Data Analysis 33
Data Collection 33
Dedication iii
Definition of Terms 21
Delimitations 22
Department of Health and Human Services 27
Dependability 32
Dissertation 5
Dissertation Coach. 67
Dissertation Content Example 23
Dissertation Format Example 112
Dissertations and Theses from Start to Finish: Psychology and Related Fields 2
Doi numbers 80
Editing 65
Effect 42
Epoché 33
Ethical Considerations 27
Ethnography 24
Exempt 29
Expletives 44
Field Test 31
Field Test Feedback Example 146
Figures 55
Findings 36, 37
Font 45
Foreword ii
Formatting 45
Gap in the Literature 15
Garner's Modern American Usage 2
generalizability 32
Geographic Location 26
Grammar assistance 80
Grounded Theory 24
Historical 24
History of the Topic 14
Hypotheses (quantitative) 25
Hypothesis 20
Impact 42
Informed Consent 26
Informed Consent for 18 Years and Over 144
Institutional Review Board 12

Institutional Review Board (IRB) Application 144
Instrumentation. 29
Journal Articles. 72
Letter of Authenticity or Originality. 144
Letter of Collaboration for Academic Institutions 144
Letter of Parental Consent for 17 Years and Younger 144
Letter of Recruitment 33, 44
Letter Of Recruitment Example. 148
Levels of Headings 45
Limitations 22
List of Possible Required Documents. 144
Lists 53
Literature Review. 14
Logical flow 16
MAXQA™ 34
McGraw-Hill Handbook of English Grammar and Usage. 1
Member Checking 34
Mentor. 7, 9
Mentoring. 73
Merriam-Webster's Collegiate Dictionary 2
Microsoft Excel. 34
Modern Language Association (MLA) Handbook for Writers of Research Papers 1
Nature of the Study. 20
Non-disclosure Agreement. 144
Non-Exempt 29
Null Hypothesis (H1⁰) .... *See* Hypothesis
Numbers. 46
NVivo™ 34
Online surveys. 80
Opinion. 47
Oral Defense Documents 144
Paragraphs. 47
Parentheses 47
Participant Withdrawal Example. 145
Participant Withdrawal form 27
Participants 47
Participatory Action Research. 25
Passive Voice. 48
Past Tense 49
Permission to Use an Existing Survey. 144
Permission to Use Archived Data. 144
Permission to Use Premises 144
Permissions 23
Permissions 30
Personification 43
Phenomenology 24

Pilot Study..30
Plagiarism...60
Population..25
Preface...iv
Presentations...73
Professional Organizations..73
Pronouns..49
Proofreaders...65
Proposal..4
Prospectus outline..12
Prospectus Outline Example...83
Publishing..71
Punctuation...49
Purpose of the Study..18
Purposive sampling...26
Qualitative...19
Quantitative...19
Quotation Mark..50
Random Sampling...26
Rationale..20
Recommendations for Future Research..38
Redundancy...50
References..32, 62
Reliability...32
Request for Non-University Committee Member...144
Research Method and Design Appropriateness...20, 24
Research Plan...12
Research Plan Example...91
Research Question(s) (RQ)...20
Research Questions...25
Resource Examples..80
Results..36
Review of the Findings...38
Review of the Problem...38
Run-on Sentences...51
Sample..25
Sampling Technique..26
Scholarly Tone...51
Scope..22
Self-referral...53
Sentence Clarity..53
Seriation...53
Significance of the Problem...19
Split infinitives..54
Statement of the Problem..18
Statistical Package for the Social Sciences™...33

Statistical Terms.. 54
Statisticians.. 68
Student Code of Conduct.. 64
Subject-Verb Agreement... 55
Sub-questions (qualitative).. 25
Summary..15, 22, 35, 39, 129, 132, 136, 137, 139, 140
Summary of the Literature... 38
Tables... 55
Teaching.. 73
The "Recipe".. 23
The Oxford Essential Guide to Writing... 2
Theoretical Framework.. 20
Theories... 15
Thesis.. 6
Those.. 57
Title Searches, Books, Articles, Research Documents, and Journals....................... 14
Topic.. 11
Transcribing... 34
Transcriptionists.. 67
Transferability.. 32
Transitions... 57
Triangulation... 32
Turnitin.. 80
Validity... 32
Verbatim Transcripts... 34
Verbs.. 58
Verb-Tense Agreement... 59
Volunteerism.. 74
Words and Phrases to Avoid Using out of Normal Context. 59
Writing Tutor... 67

62729459R00094

Made in the USA
Lexington, KY
15 April 2017